GENUINE CUISINE
OF
MAURITIUS

D1354084

GUY FÉLIX

Photos: Ronald Bégué

Published by
Editions de L'Océan Indien
Stanley, Rose-Hill
Mauritius

ISBN 99903-0-063-1

1st   Print: Singapore National Printers Ltd. (1988)
1st Reprint: Singapore National Printers Ltd. (1992)

CONTENTS

PREFACE

An invitation from Guy Félix is always welcome. It is therefore with great pleasure that I present him my best wishes of success on the occasion of the publication of his book on the Mauritian Cuisine.

Mauritius is a meeting place of different races, a melting-pot. That diversity, which constitutes our richness, is again present in our feeding habits, each ethnic group having, in the course of time, kept its tastes and cooking tradition.

Africa, Europe and Asia are all represented in our dishes as components of our mixed culture.

We must add to these foreign influences and contribution what makes up our own Creole and Indian Ocean civilisation.

All these have given birth to the Mauritian cuisine, quite specific and unique in kind, though it shares many characteristics with the cuisine of the other islands of the Indian Ocean and distant Creole countries of the Carribean and the Louisiana.

It is that genuine cuisine, the recipes of which have been handed over from generation to generation, which is presented to us by Guy Félix in his book.

Besides being a well-known theoretician in matters of cooking (Guy Félix is also the author of "Une Synthèse des cuisines Mauriciennes" published in 1972), he has proved himself to be not only a man of words but also of deeds: His actual presence in the kitchen, his constant interest in everything having to do with pots and pans testify to this, as well as his skill in practical demonstration of cooking in front of customers of a well-known departmental store.

Thanks to him, to his ideas and lively imagination, we have learnt to vary our menus, to whet our appetite, and to choose the best kitchen products.

In short we have learnt how to eat well.

This book of Guy Félix marks one of the stepping-stones in the course of that long struggle which aims at bettering the quality of life of all Mauritians without distinction.

A well-furnished table is one of the greatest pleasures of life . . . May that pleasure be shared by all our countrymen and by all the foreigners who visit us and who are thus invited to taste a genuine cuisine.

Congratulations Guy. And Bon Appétit to all of you.

Sir Gaëtan Duval

INTRODUCTION

To eat or not to eat. . . This "to be or not to be" is the dilemma which man has had to face since days unknown, when he succeeded in standing upright on his hind legs. This is the dilemma that doubtless, must have been the greatest if not the most important way forward on the road to progress. It is hunger recurring at regular and daily intervals that has goaded that small vague mist of intelligence that one day started to float somewhere within the brains in an undetermined and formless skull.

To appease that beast, that would twist his bowels, he started using his brains, to catch his prey, to fight, to pay for his errors, to putting two and two together, to prey, to make estimations and thence to start thinking. This is how Mother Nature, through some whim of her own has singularised the human being among the thousands of other mammalians and enabled him somehow to stand up on its ridiculously weak hind parts; while the main functions would develop at the other end: that is the skull where for million of years, the circumvolutions of the grey cells would grow bigger and bigger as the human being would think more and more.

Our ancestors did not fail to progress since they very soon discovered that the meat of their likes had a much better taste when roasted. It may well be that by hazard a bush of fire was lit on a hot summer day, through a terrific heat. But from then one, they endeavoured to reproduce nature and some happy day, a spark sprung from somewhere and started simultaneously hundred of events. Human beings now could start cooking. Once again it became necessary to start thinking hard through necessity. So all along innumerate centuries, from one unsuccessful to another successful ones attempted, something developed, and became what was to be an essential aspect of human life: good cooking which is according to French ladies experts in this field, the best hold on any male.

But it seems that the human race has been plagued with an unsatisfactory greed that makes man look not only forward to eat his fill, but also to eat well. An endless crusade was launched there for constant researches in the hundreds of ways of preparing one meal. And without joke, that crusade numbers its martyrs like Vatel for instance, as well as its great masters like Curnousky in modern times. I would not be able to name all the people concerned and involved in good cooking throughout the world as it is a large one and indeed the different cooking methods are all as good when studied. I have not the slightest doubt that the human hand, the best choice in that matter, when well-cooked constitutes a savoury for a cannibal, or that the large wood worms are a delicacy to the Ethiopian palate: it is all a question of latitudes and customs.

As for us, well, we are Nature's favourite children since under our own climate we have such a wide choice of cookery from so many civilisations. In that realm again, we are forced to admit that we could live happy and content. One only has to go through the index of the present volume to be convinced that the Star of the Indian Ocean, like some oyster producing its own pearl, has brought forth a greedy son who grew to be a gourmet as soon as he started tropical cooking that is Creole, Chinese, Indian or Muslim that have all crystalized under this latitude. At a look at Guy Félix, one understands immediately without any mis-quoting of the spirit of the Greek philosopher, that he is an Epicurian. Just listen to his talking of his favourite hobby: cookery and you will understand that if on the one hand, he brings relief as a physiotherapist to pain and bones, on the other hand, he does not disdain looking with great happiness after the main organ: the stomach while allowing some importance to the tongue that fleshly and mobile part without which one would be unable to taste anything.

The famous Curnousky was overheard one day, saying: "Whenever you wish to eat some savoury dish, go to some doctor or some priest." Do put into practice, this good piece of advice. A book written by a gentleman of the medical world is a must on the shelves of your cookery books. What are the chances of success? He has tried himself all the recipes he is now bringing to you and he is still alive and well alive.

Pierre Edmond Pulvenis.

Guy Félix
M.C.S.P, H.T.

Born 8th June 1937
at Petit Raffray, Mauritius.

Chief Physiotherapist,
Ministry of Health.

Demonstrator Cook
at Mammouth.

"You must eat well to work well. And you must work well to eat well, too!"

FORWARD

You may well ask what relates a physiotherapist to a first-rate cook. Rest assured there is none.

My interest for cookery, specially for the good one started while I was still a very young scout of Father Moriarty and when I started preparing different meals in the rigid conditions imposed on us by the laws of the scout movement. Later on when I attended the Royal College of Curepipe, we went to holiday camps under the guidance of Guy Chis and of old Jean Louis. How much elating and enriching were those meals we invented and which we had such pleasure in eating as we knew we had ourselves prepared them. Later on I became a student in London, and compelled by circumstances, since I was not at all prepared to allow myself to get poisoned; so I started preparing myself my meals. I well remember the day I saw Clifford Gassin, a chicken under his right arm and a bottle of "V.P. Wine" under his left, entering my room and shouting: "Matante prepare us some chicken curry."

This is how cookery has always been a subject of great interest to me. I later realised that in Mauritius, we had the possibility and the privilege of being able to taste of, and appreciate the cookery of the different communities that form the mosaic of our population. The Chinese cookery, which speaks for itself, Indian and Muslim cooking, of which the spiced meals, ally so well with our latin and tropical character and in the last the Creole cookery, which to my point of view is an out-product of all those with an adaptation of the French or European cooking. The great variety of tropical products renders us unable to say that we have not been favoured by nature. As everything in life, everything must be tried, at least once. Every human being should be able to eat whatever is pleasing to his palate and that goes through the stomach without causing ulcers, urticaria diabetes or again that illness of those who enjoy life: Gout!

In the next pages, I have attempted to attain a synthesis of those various cookings. I see no reason, why with the help of modern ages, we cannot cook on a gas fire what the great Chinese cooks "Dai See Foch" or the great Indian Bandaris would cook on a wood fire.

The great secret of Chinese cooking is to cook as rapidly as possible vegetables and certain meats. To succeed in this, it is necessary to have a very high fire and a special pan in which food does not stick to the bottom. Some of the vegetables that our grandmothers would cook for hours in conventional pans, (process that would deprive the vegetables of all their nutritive value and of their savour) can well be cooked in those Chinese woks. From the Indian cooking, we can benefit from the judicious choice of those same spices which give so much savour to everything that is cooked and that activate our salivary glands for a better digestion.

Once again, I shall stop at a synthesis of spices. I believe that with some discernment we can easily make use of the spices of the different methods. There is no reason whatsoever for not using ajinomoto to serve a (tenrec) curry or roasted grub of wasps; why not make use of the different excellent Chinese sauces to better a roasted meat or a steak.

I must admit that in many cases, I have found it difficult to classify a particular meal. I believe that already through circumstances the synthesis has already been made, and that it was only necessary to describe the process and explain it.

I shall end with these words: if we Mauritians, we cannot get together either on the political, social and economic plan, there is at least one realm in which we are forced to agree: it can only be within the gastronomical realm.

Guy Félix

SOME BITS OF MAURITIAN HISTORY

The island remained uninhabited until the end of the 18th century.

The first European visitor was probably the Portuguese navigator, Domingos Fernandez who called here in 1510.

It was the Portuguese navigator, Pedro Mascarenhas who gave his name to the group, Mauritius, Reunion Island and Rodrigues.

The only traces of their stay were the domesticated animals and the monkeys they left behind.

It was only in 1638 that the Dutch decided to occupy the island to which they gave the name of Mauritius in the honour of their sovereign, Prince Maurice.

When they left in 1710, the dodo, a kind of enormous duck had disappeared.

The island relapsed into wilderness and the Javaneese and the wild boar proliferated freely in the woods.

In 1715, Sea Captain Guillaume Dufresne D'Arsel took possession of that stop-over on the East Indian route and called it Isle de France.

Under the energetic administration of Bertrand François Mahé de Labourdonnais (1735–1746) the island started developing.

In 1810 the island was captured by the English.

In 1814, by the Treaty of Paris, the island was definitely given over by France to England and was given back its first name Mauritius or Ile Maurice.

And it was only on the 12th March 1968, that Mauritius became independent.

GEOGRAPHY

In the middle of the Indian Ocean, some 2,400 kilometres east of the African Coast, Mauritius surrounded by coral reef and an emerald sea offers the charm of its beaches and of its abrupt relief.

With its 65 kms in length and 48 kms in width, the island covers an area of 1,152 sq. kms.

In the centre a plateau of 580 m in altitude formed by basaltic mountains is a testimony of the volcanic origin of the island, like the Pieter Both, famous mountain which lowers its peak at 821 m.

The highest peak of the island remains the Piton de la Rivière Noire which reaches 827 m.

The island has a subtropical climate for the pleasure and the happiness of the tourists who will be able to sunbath all along the coast on the large sand beaches.

The variations in temperature due to the mountainous relief of the land are surprising.

In August, at 652 m of altitude the normal day temperature is 19°C and in February it can reach 23°C.

At sea level, temperature is always 5°C higher.

KITCHEN WARE

"A good tool does not necessarily turn a man into a good worker." Thus goes a popular saying. But I believe that when cookery is concerned we need a minimum of utensils to be able to cook even the poorest of meals. In the lines that follow I shall try to describe the utensils that I think necessary for a good cookery.

Fire:

To be able to cook the meals I am going to describe in this book, it is imperative to have a very ardent fire: to be convinced: Have a look in the kitchen of any Chinese restaurant and so, why not Creole and Indian meals. A very strong fire is a necessity.

Rice Cooker:

The rice-cooker is a marvel of Japanese technic.

Rice is cooked almost automatically. To vary the quality of the rice you are cooking you have only to vary the quantity of water added to the rice. For grains well seperated, less water for the same quantity of rice is needed than if well cooked rice was needed.

Pressure Cooker:

The pressure-cooker is another great invention of the century; one is able to cook just anything in a relatively short time, to economize fuel and most of all to keep all the nutritive value of the meals prepared. Now from the purely culinary point of view in the local context, the pressure cooker should be kept for the cooking of soups, of pulses, stewing meats, and other meals that need a very long cooking.

Milk Shaker or Mincer:

The mincer is a centrifuge electrical machine with knife blades which makes it possible to mash, mix or homogenise vegetables, meats, soups, fruits and other things that must be tender.

The Chinese Wok:

The Chinese wok is an essential instrument to make good cookery. It enables a regularized cooking of your meals while making it possible for the ingredients to be mixed without being crushed, and thereby a rapid evaporation of the liquid: hence a quicker thickening of the sauce. One can make use of a special spoon (called spatula), to stir the ingredients in the wok. Place the spoon on the border of the wok, scrap down then lift the spatula quickly, repeat same all round the wok.

A Big Chinese Chopping Log:

A big Chinese chopping log made out of the tamarind-tree that is known for its hard-resisting wood. The chopping-log must be of three inches thick at least and the surface need not be too polished. It has to be washed regularly in running water and with soap.

The Big Chinese Knife:

It is necessary to have two big Chinese knives, preferably of the same weight, that must be always well sharpened.

One or two small sharp knives will be also of first necessity as well as the ordinary gadgets to peel vegetables or to shape them.

Pans and Casseroles:

Pans with lids and of different sizes are also of great necessity, as well as pyrex dishes of different widths.

CREOLE CUISINE

Sausage Rougaille.
Recipe on page 19–20.

Fricassee Red Beans.
Recipe on page 27.

Curry

The word curry has a persian origin "Khurdi" meaning broth or juicy meat, and is derived from "Khurdan" meaning eat or drink.

The term can easily designate a sauce containing chilly and other spices like saffron, coriander, ginger, pepper and garlic, or again a meal of meat, fish, vegetables and any of these cooked in that sauce. The curry powder contains different spices more or less hot.

Curry is so popular that the word is now used in everyday language to mean anything that goes with rice or bread, naturally enough, purists use that word only when referring to those very spicy meals that bring water to the mouth.

There is a considerable variety of "Curries" and different ways of preparing it, but in all circumstances the secret is a judicious balance and a perfect blending of the different spices, that are indispensable to the sauce or to the powder. Invaluable to that matter, is the curry stone, that our country fellows, new Australians, have taken with them to their new fatherland. Spices that come into the composition of the paste of the powder are invariably: dried saffron and coriander; then at the connoisseur's choice: ginger, garlic, red chilly (dried), pepper, cloves (nut meg). To obtain the right proportions in the judicious balance just mentioned, is naturally a question of taste, but I would personally advise to consult the nearest shopkeeper. At request he will prepare a mixture of the proper spices but he should pack them separately, you will then be able to obtain the right proportion of a good curry that you will later be able to judge and according to your taste, you will then be in a position to make the necessary modifications.

Here are for your personal uses some indications.

Ingredients:

8 gms of turmeric (saffron)
2 tablespoonfuls of coriander
5 gms of grains of black pepper
½ gm of nutmeg
10 gms of green ginger and garlic
Chillies (to taste)

Preparation:

Roast the grains of coriander, just enough to avoid dissipating the aroma, grind the ingredients on the pounding rock or a mixer; but some practice is necessary for this pounding for the mixture must be homogenous and of a pasty consistence. The last water used for the washing of the rock must be kept.

To Brown Massala:

Curry powder, must be diluted in some warm water to form a paste, like your massala that has been crushed on the pounding rock. In each case, the browning is carried in the same way.

N.B. "Massala is the name given to the curry paste either freshly ground or the powder diluted in tepid water."

Cooking:

In a pan pour out oil with two twists of the hand; when the oil is hot, brown 10 seconds two small onions sliced very finely, then add your curry paste. Stirring constantly for another 10 seconds, add by spoonfuls the water from the grinding slab or some boiling water (in the case of the already ground curry powder), allow to brown for another 3 to 4 seconds and keep turning; your massala can be considered as to be cooked only when the oil gets separated from your massala and when by the smell, one can tell the massala is cooked; the sauce is then ready to receive your meat, your fish or your vegetables.

You will need two other ingredients to complete your sauce: tamarind and tomatoes, the first soaked in cold water and the second sliced out very thinly or homogenised, must be added during the two last minutes of the cooking while the curry is being cooked on a very low fire.

Those who like a perfumed and aromatised curry, chop finely a bunch of coriander leaves, add it at the end of the cooking, mix well and close the pan that must be opened only when ready to serve so as to titilate the salivary glands of guests.

The Monkey Curry or Curry No. 2

According to a popular saying, nothing is better than our like, and as we are supposed to have monkey ancestors it follows that the meat we should appreciate mostly should be the monkey's. In fact, I consider that the monkey's meat is the best game meat to be had: A scientific analysis has proved beyond doubt that the monkey's meat contains first class protein and no cholesterol at all. It can be prepared in three different ways: in a curry sauce, stew or (in rolls). But only the curry can give the whole savour of the monkey's meat.

Ingredients:

A monkey (³/₄ kg of meat)
50 gms of massala
3 small onions
2 tamarind balls
1 bunch of coriander
Oil

For the Marinade:

6 small onions chopped finely
1 tablespoonful of ground garlic and ginger
1 small teaspoonful of ground cloves
1 small teaspoonful of ground cinnamon
1 teaspoonful of ajinomoto
3 leaves of curry leaves
1 teaspoonful of ground pepper
2 teaspoonfuls of table oil
2 teaspoonfuls of white wine

The preparation of the monkey's meat

It is much better to use the monkey that has been killed at hunting. Tie and hang the animal by the legs, cut the skin round the neck and wrists and pull off the fur. Take out the bowels and wash thoroughly. Take out all the bones with a very sharp knife, then cut the meat into slices of 2 cm cube. Allow this meat to marinade for some 5–6 hours in the above listed ingredients.

Cooking:

As the meat needs sometime of cooking, it is preferable to use a pressure cooker.

Have some 60 gms of massala ground on the grinding slab, taking care to keep the last water of the rock. Slice 3 small onions. Let 2 tamarind balls in ½ cup of hot water and take out the seeds.

Pour oil with three twists of oil into your pressure cooker. When the oil is very hot, brown the onions, then add the massala, turning vigorously all the time. Add water obtained from the grinding slab mixed with the tamarind. Stir. The massala is cooked when the oil is separated from the massala. Pour in the monkey's meat, stir, and gradually add the marinade's sauce. Mix well the massala and the meat. Allow to cook, then close your pressure cooker and wait for the first whistle. At the first whistle, turn down the fire and let the meat simmer for 30 minutes if the monkey was a young one or 45 minutes if it was an old-fellow.

Slice very finely a bunch of coriander, leaves, open your pressure cooker, put in your coriander, mix and close again. Turn down the fire. The cooker must not be opened until ready to serve, as the coriander leaves constitute the best stimulating aroma.

Pork Curry and Pigeon Peas

Ingredients:

1 kg of pork

½ kg of pigeon peas

100 gms of freshly ground massala

Ground ginger, garlic, salt, pepper and ajinomoto

2 Bombay onions

6 fine tomatoes

Oil

Preparation:

Dice your pork and mix with salt, pepper and ajinomoto. Bring water to boil in a pan; at the boiling point, put in your peas for 2 minutes and drain.

Cooking:

Pour some oil in a pressure cooker. Brown your onions, together with ginger and garlic, brown the meat for 2 minutes, add the massala, let the meat brown in the massala for 2 minutes, put in the peas, brown for 2 minutes, add the crushed tomatoes. Close the pressure cooker and allow to cook for 10 minutes.

Jack Fruit and Pork Curry

The jack fruit is one of those tropical fruits that are delicious fruits when ripe and delicious vegetables when tender. The success of your meal will depend on the choice of the fruit. It must be absolutely tender and young; the best choice is that of the fruit called "Jack la boue" or "Gluey Jack" for the best curry.

Ingredients:

A small jack fruit of 1–1½ kg

½ kg of pork (½ lean and ½ fat)

150 gms of freshly ground massala

Ground garlic and ginger

Finely chopped onions, salt, pepper and ajinomoto

2 Bombay onions

6 fine tomatoes

Oil

Preparation:

With a big knife, cut into four the jack fruit and with a small knife, peel off the thick skin and cut the fruit into small pieces which must be placed immediately into cold water. Dice also the pork, add salt, pepper and ajinomoto.

Cooking:

Pour with two twists of the hand, oil in a pressure cooker. Brown your Bombay onions chopped finely. Add the ginger and the garlic. Cook until brown. Add the pork, cook to brown for another 2 minutes, add a spoonful of water, close the cooker and allow to cook for some 12 minutes, from the time of the first whistle. Open, take out the pork and keep it warm. Add some oil, if necessary let the small onion brown as well as the massala. You can brown the spices with a spoon-ful of the pork juice and as soon as the oil and the massala get separated, put in your pork and allow to cook for 2 minutes while stirring continuously. Then add your jack fruit, let it brown for some 2 more minutes, add your tomatoes, and some salt if necessary, close your pressure cooker and cook for another 10 minutes.

Serve with rice and a tomoto chutney.

Dholl, Drum Stick and Salted Fish Curry

Ingredients (for 6):

3 measures from the rice-cooker of dholl

2 bundles of drum sticks as tender as possible

125 gms of freshly ground mixture of curry (massala paste) OR

3 tablespoonfuls of curry powder diluted in some warm water

1 tablespoonful of garlic and ginger

3 small onions finely sliced

6 fine tomatoes (crushed)

2 tamarind balls melted into ½ cup of warm water

Salt, pepper and ajinomoto (to taste)

12 pieces of salted fish

Oil

Preparation & Cooking:

Pour two twists of the oil into a pressure cooker. Deep-fry your salted fish until a pink colour, take it out and place it in a bowl. Add some more oil if necessary, brown your pepper, onions, the massala paste, stirring continuously, until the oil and the massala get separated, put in the drum sticks, and allow to brown for some 2 more minutes, then add your dholl; cook for some minutes adding all the tamarind water in which ajinomoto will have been diluted. Add boiling water to fill half of your pot, close and allow to cook for some 15 more minutes from the first whistle. Steam off, put in your salted fish, cook for 3 minutes on a reduced heat.

Serve with a fine, grained rice and a coconut chutney. Some gourmets replace the drum sticks by the chocho. The chocho or egg-fruit must then be served very tender, peeled and cut into four pieces.

Ashgourd and Beef Tripe

Among the curries called mixed curries i.e. meat and vegetables, the ashgourd curry and beef tripe is in a very good position on my list of the choicest meals, for different reasons: as the ashgourd and tripes are very inexpensive and secondly because the ashgourd is a very nutritive vegetable although it has a very insipid taste when cooked otherwise.

Ingredients:

1 kg of young and tender ashgourds

1 kg of white tripes (deep frozen)

6 tomatoes

1 tablespoonful of garlic and ginger

4 chopped onions

Salt, pepper and ajinomoto

2 tablespoonfuls of curry powder diluted into some tepid water, or else freshly ground massala

Oil

Preparation:

Allow your tripes to thaw, clean them thoroughly, cut them into small pieces, add salt, pepper and ajinomoto. Put some oil in your pressure cooker, brown ½ of your onions, add the tripes, allow for some 5 minutes, add a soup ladle of hot water, then close the cooker. At the first whistle, turn down the fire and cook for another 30 minutes.

In the meantime, halve your ashgourds, empty them, cut them into fine "comas" and immerse them into slightly salted water. Rinse and drain.

Cooking:

In a Chinese wok, pour 4 twists of oil (for the ashgourd absorbs a lot of oil). Brown pepper and put in your ashgourd; with the Chinese spatula, stir continuously and fry for some 10 minutes, until your gourd has acquired a nice yellow colour. Take your gourd out of the fire and keep it warm in a bowl.

If necessary put some oil in a wok, brown the rest of onions, ginger and garlic, add curry paste, stirring continuously.

Add some water from the tripes, that will probably be oily and greasy. Allow to brown until the oil and the turmeric get separated. Then add your tripes, cook for another 3 to 4 minutes. Put in your tomatoes cut into 4. Cover your wok with a wooden lid, allow to simmer for some minutes, add the gourd and stir. After some minutes the gourd should have taken its original form.

Unicorn Fish Curry and Bitter Gourd

Ingredients:

A small licorn of 1 kg

½ kg of bitter gourd very green

4–5 tomatoes

125 gms crushed massala, garlic, ginger, minced onions, salt, pepper and tamarind

1 bunch of coriander

Oil

Preparation:

Peel off the fish, empty and cut into slices add salt and pepper, and deep fry them, turning them over from time to time. Take them out of the oil and keep them in a warm place. Seive the oil to take out the bits and pieces.

Cut your gourds lengthwise, with a spoon, peel off the interior that comes out easily. Cut your gourd into 2 and 4 pieces for each gourd. Wash thoroughly, add salt to gourd and after 10 minutes wash and drain.

Cooking:

Pour two twists of oil in a Chinese wok, fry the gourds for some 5 minutes, stirring from time to time, cover and allow to cook for 2 minutes. Uncover to stir and cover again quickly. Take out the gourds and keep warm. In the oil, cook a curry sauce as already indicated. Put your fish in that sauce for some 5 minutes and the gourds for the last 2 minutes, add some coriander leaves minced. Mix and cover.

Serve with rice and clear soup of drum stick leaves.

Tenrec Curry or Madagascar Hedgehog

The tenrec or madagascar hedgehog is an animal that lives six months on land and the six winter months wintering. The hunt for the hedgehog starts traditionally the 1st of May. Will go on for only a few weeks as the hedgehog will then go wintering around mid-April and is naturally at that precise moment, very fat, it will be so lean afterwards that it will be of no use. Connoisseurs will tell you that the male has much more taste that the female, hunters usually beat it on the head and make use of the dog, a specialist for that kind of hunting.

Ingredients:

1 tenrec

1 tablespoonful salpeter

2 small onions

125 gms of curry powder or freshly ground massala

Some tomatoes

For Marinade:

2 minced Bombay onions

1 tablespoonful of ground garlic, ginger, salt, pepper and ajinomoto

1 pinch of powdered cinnamon

1 pinch of powdered cloves

Some bay leaves

A few curry leaves

10 cl white wine

2 tablespoonfuls oil

1 teaspoonful salt

Preparation:

Plunge the hedgehog into boiling water for some minutes. Using a very sharp knife or if necessary a razor, scrape out the fur. Cut off the head and the paws. Open the belly and pull out the bowels and the throat organs. Wash thoroughly in clean water. To prevent your hedgehog from smelling, remove the small bone at the end of the spine, that is the one before the tail (sexual glands). Cut the animal into pieces and wash out the parts in clean water, put them into a plate, and later rub the pieces with salpeter and place them into a cool section of your refrigerator. In the meantime prepare your marinade by mixing the listed ingredients. After an hour or so, remove your tenrec from refrigerator. Wash and drain. Then mix well in marinade and leave for 6 hours.

Cooking:

Pour out some oil into a pressure cooker, brown 2 minced onions, add the freshly ground massala, allow to brown for some minutes, using your massala water to moisten your sauce, add pieces of hedgehog, simmer for 5 minutes, add some minced tomatoes, brown then, add all the marinade sauce and allow to cook for 20 minutes. You should then be able to serve with rice and chilly (Grand malice sauce).

As the meat of the hedgehog has a very strong smell, use more spices adding if necessary more chillies to the massala.

Roasted Tenrec or Madagascar Hedgehog

Ingredients:

1 tenrec

Margarine

1 teaspoonful honey

For Marinade:

2 minced Bombay onions

1 tablespoonful of ground garlic, ginger, salt, pepper and ajinomoto

1 pinch of powdered cinnamon

1 pinch of powdered cloves

Some bay leaves

A few curry leaves

10 cl white wine

2 tablespoonfuls oil

1 teaspoonful salt

Preparation:

Prepare your hedgehog as for the curry, do not cut it into pieces. Leave it whole and allow to marinade in a large plate.

Cooking:

Take it out, drain, attach together the paws, apply margarine all round the beast. Fold into a large tin foil paper. Put some margarine here and there first on the paper, folding in the large sides before the small ones. Warm your oven, place the animal in the middle, cook for 10 minutes, reduce the heat, and allow to cook for another 50 minutes. Open the oven and the foil paper, taking care not to spill the sauce. Put 2 tablespoonfuls of this hot sauce in a bowl, melt a teaspoonful of honey. Pour over the roasted animal this sauce. Foil in again and place back into the oven for another 10 minutes and a little more if necessary if the meat is not cooked enough.

Use a fork to find out whether the meat is cooked.

Roasted Beef Tongue

Ingredients:

1 kg of beef tongue

2 Bombay onions

*1 tablespoonful of ground garlic
and ginger*

12 garlic pods

*Salt, pepper, ajinomoto, siaw sauce,
nutmeg, cloves powder and "Heung
New Fun" (Chinese spices)*

1 teaspoonful honey

Oil

Preparation:

Take the beef tongue, plunge into boiling water, then with a sharp knife, take out the skin that covers the tongue: but it may be necessary to put back the tongue into hot water to clean everything.

Melt a spoonful of ajinomoto in a spoonful of siaw sauce. Take a large injection syringe, pump the siaw sauce and with a big needle inject that solution here and there in different parts of the tongue, take out the needle.

Using a very sharp knife, insert a garlic pod into the meat, repeat the operation several times, until you have used up all the garlic pods. Make a mixture of all the spices left, rub the tongue with it.

Cooking:

Pour out two twists of oil into the pressure cooker, brown for 10 seconds 2 minced Bombay onions; put in the beef tongue and allow to brown on all sides; then add some hot water to cover half the meat; close the lid and allow to cook for some 30 minutes. Then open the lid and using a fork, find out whether the meat is cooked. Take out the tongue from the cooker, pour some more oil into the cooker, melt some honey into the sauce and pour this mixture on the tongue that you will have to put back into the cooker, turning from time to time to brown on all sides.

Roasted Pork

Roasted pork is said to be very heavy but there is one way of rendering it more digestive on the condition of not eating too much!

Ingredients:

1 kg of pork without bone

2 tablespoonfuls of margarine

1 tablespoonful of ground mustard

75 cl of hot milk

3/4 minced onions

Some garlic pods and some garlic and ginger

Salt, ajinomoto, pepper, nutmeg, cloves, siaw sauce and honey

Oil

Preparation:

Put the garlic pods in the pork using a sharp pointed knife, and then season it with the spices in the following order: garlic and ginger, salt, pepper, nutmeg, cloves, apply margarine generously on the interior and exterior. Roll and tie the pork with a piece of string.

Cooking:

Pour some hot oil in a pressure cooker, brown the onions and put in the pork. Brown on all sides turning with a big fork. When your pork is brown, add the boiling milk and close the cooker. Allow to cook for some 1¼ hours. Open your cooker, take the pork out of the sauce and put back the cooker on the fire with some oil. Add a spoonful of siaw and a spoonful of honey. Put back the pork and brown for some minutes. Your meat will then have the beautiful brown colour you can see on the roasted pork in the window shop of Port-Louis.

Roasted Fowl

Ingredients:

A young fowl of 1 kg (fresh)

Salt, pepper, ajinomoto, Heung New Fun, nutmeg, cloves, cinnamon, margarine, siaw sauce, and a teaspoonful of honey.

Preparation:

Clean the fowl in the Chinese fashion (as described in the Chinese section). Wash and if necessary, put the fowl over a flame to burn out the small feathers. Apply on the interior as well as the exterior, a mixture of all the spices in powder form, then margarine, spraying well all the surface of the fowl; place thyme and parsley inside and attach the fowl with a string. Wrap in an alluminium foil sheet.

Cooking:

Place the fowl in the very hot oven for 10 minutes, then on a medium one for another 20 minutes. Then open the foil, take out 2 spoonfuls of the juice, mix with some siaw, honey and pinch of "Heung New Fun" and sprinkle, the fowl with this sauce. Allow to cook for another 10 minutes. You can turn over the fowl in the paper and you won't have to close it again.

The Barbecue

During the last years, with the fear of cholesterol, grilled meat has become the latest fashion. The main idea being that as the meat is grilled, the fat is burnt away leaving only proteins. In any case, with the help of modern ideas, the barbecue is in great demand on the island. One can see along the sea coast, all sorts of device to grill meat. Some very elaborate and costly apparatus do exist to grill the meat of the chicken or that of the suckling pig. In the following lines, I shall endeavour to describe some small apparatus that with the help of your imagination, will enable you to grill the meat to your choice.

In principle, all grilled meats should be done on charcoal; some connoisseurs will tell you that the best is probably the charcoal made of the eucalyptus tree, but I can assure you that this is not necessary; you can as well make use of a very dry wood, as the smoke coming from green wood is very disagreeable, and gives a very bad taste to the meat.

There are two sorts of barbecue: one for which the pieces of meat, as for the chicken are cut before being grilled (Pork cuttlets or chops are also very good for barbecue). And of course there is still the traditional way of grilling which is to put on the spit the chicken or the suckling pig and to roast them over the fire.

Preparation for the meats:

Very tender meat is necessary for the barbecue, as it is necessary that the meat keeps its taste.

RECIPE FOR 4 CHICKENS OF 1 KG

Ingredients:

For the sauce:

4 tablespoonfuls of siaw

4 tablespoonfuls of honey

2 teaspoonfuls of ajinomoto

2 teaspoonfuls of pepper powder

2 teaspoonfuls margarine

Preparation:

Cut your chicken in big pieces, according to the conventional way. Make a sauce with all the mentioned ingredients, mix well with the pieces of chicken and allow to macerate for about 6 hours.

Cooking:

Light your charcoal fire, but never put on your meat as long as the charcoal is smoking. Melt a small tin of margarine. Using a brush, apply thickly on the pieces of meat the melted margarine and then place the pieces of meat on the grill for some minutes; drops of grease of either the margarine or of the meat will be falling in your fire re-animating it; this is however, important, since this is what will give taste to your meat. If on the other side, the fire becomes too strong take out some embers or at the best spray it with some water, (a small trick is to use an empty shampoo plastic bottle). To make sure that your meat is cooked, normally the appetizing golden colour should be enough, but you can also use a fork, if it goes straight in your meat, it should be cooked.

To cook whole chickens, it is not necessary, to let them macerate in the sauce for a long time, for the cooking on a spit will take you some time and will give you probably much more enjoyment.

After cleaning thoroughly your chicken, rub it with the mixture of siaw, honey, ajinomoto, pepper on the inside and on the outside, put some margarine in the breast, place it on the spit, tie it and turn it continuously while smearing it from time to time, with melted margarine. You must make sure that the fire is not too strong as the interior of the chicken must be cooked. You must allow one hour for the cooking of your chicken, a suckling pig will need 2 hours or more.

Suckling Pig

Ingredients:

1 suckling pig

2 tablespoonfuls of salpetre

2 teaspoonfuls of sugar

2 tablespoonfuls of margarine

Salt, siaw, pepper, honey and ajinomoto

Preparation & Cooking:

Buy a small pig that has not eaten anything solid. Kill it by piercing it through the heart, open the belly and take out all the bowels and the thorax organs, plunge it in scalding water, rub out completely the hide, wash in cold water and wipe thoroughly with paper towels. Using 2 spoonfuls of salpetre, rub your pig on the inside as well as on the outside. Leave for 2 hours in your refrigerator. Wash it and then rub it with a mixture of siaw, honey, ajinomoto and pepper. After 2 hours put it on the spit, and tie it. It is not necessary to use a large quantity of margarine as the pig has naturally lots of fat, and should cook in its own fat, but you can use from time to time some margarine. To obtain a golden appetizing colour, just before it is completely cooked, melt some sugar in margarine, smear the beast with that mixture and cook for some more minutes. Your meat will be more tasty if it is cooked for some time on a low fire, which will be the pretext for more cocktails during the long cooking.

The suckling pig is served with roasted potatoes and lettuce salad.

Brochettes

Brochettes are small cubes of meat broiled on long iron or wooden spits that are grilled on the fire for some time. Charcoal stoves should be the best solution. You can also use wheel spokes, or an umbrella's ribs or again bamboo sticks washed thoroughly.

Schish Kabab

Ingredients:

1 kg of tender pork
1 tin of cocktail sausages
½ kg of boiling bacon
½ kg of green peppers
½ kg of Bombay onions
Siaw sauce, honey, ajinomoto and pepper
100 gms of margarine
2 heads of lettuce
Worcester sauce or special barbecue sauce

Preparation & Cooking:

Cut the tender pork meat and boiling bacon into dices. Cut into pieces the green peppers and Bombay onions.

Blend some siaw, honey, ajinomoto and pepper. Put your pieces of pork meat and boiling bacon into this sauce for at least 1 hour.

Place on the spit alternatively a piece of meat, a piece of onion, a piece of boiling bacon, small sausage and a piece of green pepper. Spread evenly with a pastry brush melted margarine and cook on small embers, turning from time to time. When the brochette is cooked after some 10 minutes, take it out with a fork and place on a plate of lettuce. Serve with worcester sauce or garlic Chinese sauce or again the special French barbecue sauce.

Note that veal liver, veal heart, bacon, raw ham diced serve very well in brochettes.

Fried Wasp Grub with Bombay Onions

There is in Mauritius a common insect that goes by the name of "Yellow Wasp" or wasp (the scientific name being Polistes Herbraus). It exists at one moment of its life cycle in a grub form and is generally found laid within a sort of comb that is produced by the adult insect. Those combs can be seen at the top of trees. To pick the combs (children are particularly good at that game), one must use a long stick at the end of which are attached old pieces of cloth set to flame. The smoke afright the adult insects. When the adults are really gone and this is very important, since a wasp bite is everything but interesting, a blow with the stick on the comb, makes the latter fall. I can only hope for you that the comb will be full of grub.

Ingredients:

1 large comb of wasp
2 big Bombay onions
2 twists of oil
1 tablespoonful of vinegar
1 teaspoonful of siaw sauce
½ teaspoonful of ajinomoto

Preparation:

Pass the comb over a flame, knock lightly with the palm of the hand, the grub will fall on a plate. The grub must be sorted out and only the larva kept because some may have started changing into adults.

Place the larva into a bowl.

Add a teaspoonful of ajinomoto, another of siaw sauce. Mix well.

Mince finely the big onions (Bombay type).

Cooking:

Put oil with two twist of hand in a Chinese wok.

Put the grub into a hot oil, stirring continuously for 2 minutes. Make a hole in the midst of the grub and place the onions. Fry for some 30 seconds and then stir constantly for another 2 minutes. Before retrieving from the fire, add a spoonful of white vinegar and stir again.

Serve hot with nicely cooked rice and possibly with a hot chillie sauce.

An excellent meal would be rice, fried wasp grub, a vegetable fricassee or boiled pulses.

Remark:

Wasp grubs contain a high proportion of protein.

Rougaille

Rougaille is another of these Creole courses that find the favour of the Mauritian housewife. The reason is to be found in the fact that it is so easily cooked, is so very well appreciated, very digest and serve nicely with a good number of rice courses.

The word itself is supposed to derive from 2 words: roux-d'ail; in other words the browning of the garlic sauce; in the same way vindaye is supposed to derive from: vin d'ail or garlic wine.

The basic element in the rougaille is the tomato. Tomatoes in Mauritius are really, love apples, rather than European tomatoes. They are also more tasty.

It is interesting to note that our friends from La Réunion use the word rougaille what we ourselves call chutney. (Basically, chutney, more particularly, tomato chutney is made out of uncooked tomatoes or at least scalded or very lightly grilled) on the contrary, they call chutney what we call rougaille. But this is only part of the Creole charm.

RECIPE FOR A GOOD ROUGAILLE

Ingredients:

3 finely chopped onions

1 tablespoonful of ginger and garlic pounded, in the mortar

Some salt, pepper and ajinomoto

1 tablespoonful of tomato paste

250 gms of red tomatoes

1 pinch of ground red chilly

For a hot rougaille use 4 big pepper, slit lengthwise

Thyme and parsley (1 bunch)

Oil

Preparation:

Put your tomatoes into scalding water, peel them and fork the tomatoes. You can also pierce the tomatoes and thus extract the grains. But you can save the trouble in using an homogenizer that in a few seconds renders your tomatoes into a paste with no grains or skins.

Cooking:

Pour out two twists of oil into a wok. When the oil is very hot, brown the pepper and the red chilly powder. Add the ground ginger and garlic, stirring continuously, then put in the onions and fry until golden; put in 1 spoonful of tomato paste, stirring continuously for 30 seconds, put in the thyme without its stem (stalk) stir for 2 seconds and adding the green peppers, brown for 10 seconds add the crushed tomatoes and stir for 10 seconds, cover with the wooden lid and leave on a moderate heat for 5 minutes. Uncover, add some hot water, ajinomoto and chopped parsley. Stir for another 10 seconds, and your sauce is ready to take in anything you may wish to put in.

The meat and fish rougaille should normally be done with fried fish or meat. To have a tastier sauce, make use of the oil in which the meat or the fish has been fried, but this oil must be used, the very day.

Sausage Rougaille

Ingredients

½ kg of sausages

Preparation & Cooking:

The secret in the cooking of sausages is to cook them on the lowest heat, so that all the fat escapes. Using a frying pan with a lid, towel dry and pour very little oil. Put in you sausages, taking care not to separate them at this stage, put them in the pan, turn them once or twice so that they are well smeared with oil; prick with a fork the sausage skin, put a lid over your pan, over a very low heat, every 10 minutes, turn over your sausages and if they tend to burst, pierce to allow the oil out, cover again and allow to cook. Your sausages should be ready when they take that pinkish tint. For sausage of medium size allow 30 minutes on a very low heat and with the fat you should be able to cook your rougaille. Put in your sausages in the rougaille sauce for 5 minutes, to enable them to take a good shape.

Serve the sausage rougaille with cooked rice and red or white boiled beans.

Rougaille of Salted Fish (Snoek)

Ingredients:

½ kg of salted fish
All ingredients for a good rougaille

Preparation & Cooking:

Cut your salted fish and soak into cold water for 20 minutes, changing the water at least once. Drain completely in a colander. Pour out two twists of oil in a wok. Fry on a medium heat the pieces of salted fish. Take them out and set aside and keep warm. In the remaining oil, cook your rougaille and put the pieces of fish in the sauce only for the last 5 minutes.

Typical Ingredients
for good Rougaille.

Corned Beef Rougaille

Ingredient:

1 tin of corned beef

Preparation & Cooking:

Prepare your sauce as indicated. Open your tin, crush the meat and add the meat only for the last 5 minutes.

Salted Meat Rougaille

Ingredient:

250 gms of salted meat

Preparation & Cooking:

Dice the meat, soak the dices in tepid water for 15 minutes, changing the water frequently. Fry them for 10 minutes on medium heat and cook in the sauce for 10 minutes. You can also add 2 green quartered peppers.

Bacon Rougaille

Ingredients:

250 gms of bacon
2 green peppers

Preparation & Cooking:

Fry the bacon on medium heat for 4 to 5 minutes, take them out and keep in a warm place. In the remaining fat, cook your rougaille sauce and put in the bacon for 5 minutes. Add the quartered pepper.

Bombay Duck Rougaille

Ingredients:

250 gms of Bombay duck
All ingredients for a good rougaille

Preparation & Cooking:

Prepare the rougaille sauce as indicated. Wash thoroughly the fish, taking out the head and the backbone. Grill it for some minutes on a charcoal fire. Then put in the sauce for at least 10 minutes.

Beef Meat Rougaille

Ingredients:

½ kg of beef meat
All ingredients for a good rougaille

Preparation & Cooking:

Slice finely your meat, batting it with the bundle of your Chinese knife, smear with pepper and starch on each slice, leave it for 15 minutes. Put some oil in the pressure cooker over a medium heat, brown 1 chopped Bombay onion until soft and translucid, put in the meat, brown on both sides, add a spoonful of hot water and cook under pressure for 10 minutes. Make your sauce using the meat juice to moisten the tomatoes. Let your meat in that sauce for 5 minutes. Add red pepper.

Stew of Green Turtle Meat

Green turtle meat is a very tasty meat containing high proportion of iron and calcium and is eaten by people who for religious reasons do not eat beef or pork.

Ingredients:

1/2 kg of green turtle meat (avoiding the green part which is the grease)

4 to 5 fine tomatoes

2 Bombay onions

1 tablespoonful of ground ginger and garlic

1 small glass of wine,

1 small glass of Martini

Ground cloves and cinnamon, mixed herbs, salt, pepper, ajinomoto (4 spices) or bay leaves

2 tablespoonfuls olive oil

Preparation:

Slice finely the meat, put the slices in a dish, put in salt, leave for 15 minutes, add all the mentioned spices, 1/2 glass of wine and 2 tablespoonfuls of olive oil, blend everything together. Marinade for 6 to 8 hours.

Cooking:

Pour out two twists of oil into a casserole, when hot brown 2 finely chopped onions, take out the pieces of meat of the sauce and put them in the casserole, stirring all the time to brown for 5 minutes. Then add the marinade, keep on the simmer, you can dilute 1 spoonful of corn flour into the sauce to give it more consistence. Some minutes before serving add your glass of martini and the rest of your glass of wine.

Serve with a lettuce salad, pieces of bread fried in butter.

Pig's Head Salami

Ingredients:

1 head of pork, washed thoroughly and shaved

3 big roughly chopped onions

1 faggot of herbs: bay leaf, sprig of thyme and parsley

Bits of cinnamon

Some cloves

1 teaspoonful of ajinomoto

1 teaspoonful of ground pepper

1 teaspoonful of table salt.

For decoration:

Boiled eggs

Gherkins

Preparation & Cooking:

Halve the head of pork lengthwise. Have it soaked in cold icy water for 2 hours. Then wash thoroughly the pork head, place it flat in a deep pan, put just enough water to cover it. Put all the spices mentioned. Cook on low heat for 3 hours. When your pork is well cooked, take it out of the water, put on a big Chinese wooden chopping slab. Take out all the bones, mince the meat with a big Chinese knife. Place the meat in a clean piece of cloth, preferably some muslin and with the help of someone twist the cloth to extract all the juice that can be had. You will keep this juice in the fridge. Butter a plate and decorate it with slices of boiled eggs and gherkins. Put in the meat tightly packed and pour on some gelatine. Place in the fridge for one night. Take out the dish the next day, slice it and serve as appetizer or hors d'oeuvre with lettuce salad.

Potted Rabbit

Ingredients:

A rabbit of about 1½ kg

½ kg of fat bacon or salted meat

½ kg of sausages

2 eggs

Carrots and onions in slices

Spices:

15 gms of table-salt

30 grains of coriander

1 spoonful of pepper

1 bunch of thyme

2 bay leaves

2 cloves

4 garlic pods

Preparation & Cooking:

Bone the rabbit and cut the meat into pieces of about 1 cm. Mince together garlic, cloves, coriander, salt, pepper, bay leaves, thyme and rub the meat with this mixture. Mince also the remains of meat. Peel the sausage. Mix up this farcemeat with two eggs and mix with a cup of cold water. Use an earthware pot, cover the bottom and the sides with bacon rashers. Then put one layer of the farcemeat, then one layer of rabbit meat and spray with a spoon of cognac or of "Bourbognac". Repeat this until the ingredients are finished, take care to finish with a layer of farcemeat. Then put on a layer of slices of carrots and onions. Cover with a layer of bacon or lard. Cover the pot and seal the lead with a flour paste. Leave in the fridge for 24 hours. The next day, place the pot in the oven at a moderate heat for 3½ hours. When the pot will be still warm, remove the layer of fat, carrots, onions and while the contents is still warm, pour over a cup of gelatine diluted in hot water. Allow to rest, cover and place in the fridge. Serve only the next day.

You can do the same recipe with the monkey meat.

Pulses

Pulses are among the favourite meals of the Mauritian housewife. They are easy to cook and accompany nearly all the curries and tomato sauces of the Mauritian cookery. There is a great variety and they have all a great nutritive value, specially in proteins.

Red and Black lentils, dholl, red, white, pink and broad beans, all the varieties of peas, pigeon peas. But as nearly all of them requires prolonged cooking, it is preferable to cook them in the pressure-cooker; Before cooking the beans, peas and even the lentils, it is necessary to allow them to soak some hours in warm water.

The following scheme will give you an idea of the time required for the cooking from the first whistle of the cooker, and from the moment you will have to reduce the heat:

BLACK LENTILS	15 — 20 MINS
RED LENTILS	12 — 15 MINS
DHOLL	15 MINS
RED/WHITE BEANS	25 — 30 MINS
PINK BEANS	12 — 15 MINS
LARGE PEAS	35 — 40 MINS
SMALL PEAS	20 MINS

The white pulses, like large peas, white peas, and dholl or the pigeon peas can be seasoned with curry. You need only brown the saffron with the onions (as for an ordinary curry) before putting in the cooked or uncooked pulses.

The Red beans have a very nice taste when cooked with the bone from a ham for a long time. Beef tripes or pig trotters also accommodate very well broad beans and can constitute at the same time a very economical and complete meal, while the dholl can be cooked easily with salted fish.

Fricassee Dholl/Red or Black Lentils

Ingredients (for 6):

2 measures of red or black lentils or dholl (soak in lukewarm water for 1 hour)

2 finely chopped onions

1 spoonful of ground garlic and ginger

Some salt, pepper and ajinomoto

125 gms of salted meat or pig skin or pig trotters

Oil

Cooking:

Pour out 1 turn of oil in the pressure cooker. Brown the salted meat diced, with pepper for 4 to 5 minutes. Add the onions, garlic and ginger and brown for 1 more minute. Then add the red or black lentils or the dholl, that you will have washed thoroughly. Allow to brown while stirring constantly for 2 minutes. Then add boiling water to fill ½ of your cooker, add ajinomoto. Add some more salt, if necessary; cover and cook on moderate heat for 15 to 20 minutes, from the first whistle. The pink beans can be cooked in exactly the same way. For some pulses that are harder to cook, it may be advisable to cook them in water before browning them.

The exact time for the cooking varies according to the quality of the pulses and the heat used to cook.

Pink beans are half-dried red beans.

Salad made from the rest of White Beans

Ingredients:

2 tablespoonfuls of salad oil

1 tablespoonful of white vinegar

2 small finely chopped onions

Some thyme and parsley

Pepper

Preparation:

Take a bowl, put in some pepper, 2 spoonfuls of salad oil, a spoonful of white vinegar, 2 small finely chopped onions, some thyme and parsley. Mix everything and mix in the rest of the white beans. This can serve very well with a roasted beef, for instance. You can use in the same way the rest of other pulses: black lentils, red beans etc.

The rest of pulses must however, be kept in the fridge to keep their taste.

Stewed Chinese Cabbage (Petsai)

Ingredients:

A fine petsai of which the leaves are green and the stalks white

125 gms of salted meat or bacon (diced)

1 tablespoonful of garlic and ginger paste

2 to 3 small chopped onions

Salt, pepper and ajinomoto

Oil

Preparation:

Cut into shreds the petsai and leave in a pan of salted water, to get rid of the small worms that can be numerous in that kind of vegetable. Then wash the leaves thoroughly and drain.

Cooking:

Pour out two turns of oil in a Chinese wok. Brown with pepper the salted meat or the bacon. While stirring continuously, add the onions and allow to brown for 10 seconds, add the vegetable and at the last minute, the garlic and the ginger. After mixing the vegetable with the meat, cover with a wooden lid. Stew for 5 minutes, with the steam evaporating the aroma of the garlic and of the ginger will come out. After 5 minutes, uncover and mix, if necessary allow the water to evaporate.

For those who like the petsai served in stock, you can add stock midway of the cooking and allow to cook for 5 more minutes.

Serve with rice and a good "rougaille" of sausages.

Stewed Dasheen Leaves

The dasheen has long violet stalk and green leaves. There exists another variety, the stalk of which is of a light green colour and that is called the white dasheen. That variety causes itching and should not therefore be consumed. On the contrary, the violet dasheen is an excellent vegetable that is a wonderful antidote for smoking. Let the smokers take the advice.

Ingredients:

1 kg of dasheen leaves

Salt and pepper to taste

2 finely chopped onions

2 balls of tamarind (dissolved in warm water)

4 pieces (50 gms) of salted fish or 1 tin of sardines or 4 bacon rashes

2 twists of oil

1 teaspoonful of pounded ginger and garlic

Some warm water

Preparation:

Buy 1 kg of young and tender dasheen leaves. Cut the stalks into bits of 5 cms, and peel off the skins that usually come out by themselves; if the leaves are tender, you can include them.

Cooking:

Put the leaves and stalks into cold water with some salt. When they are cooked, i.e. after 5 minutes of pressure cooking, drain. Pour out two twists of oil into a pan, brown some pepper, pieces of salted meat or diced bacon for some minutes, add a spoonful of ground ginger and garlic. Brown for 20 seconds, then add 2 finely chopped onions for 10 seconds. Then add your dasheen well drained, mix well, cover your casserole with a wooden lid. Cook for 5 minutes. Some minutes before taking the pan out of the fire, add the juice of two tamarind balls that you will have diluted into some warm water.

Serve with rice and a salted fish rougaille.

N.B. You can replace the tamarind by 1 spoonful of white vinegar. It is very important to put in the tamarind or the vinegar, to avoid this acid taste characteristic of the dasheen.

Egg-Plant Fricassee (Stir Frying)

Vegetables fricassee can be served with a meat or fish dish and rice/bread and are easily consumed.

There are different ways of cooking a fricassee, some people like the vegetables to be mashed. As for myself, I find that to have a tastier meal, one should proceed this way; that is the Chinese way of cooking (stir frying), to keep as much as possible the vegetable crisp, but well cooked. The vegetables must be cooked in a Chinese wok. It is necessary in almost all cases to brown some salted meat or bacon to give more taste to the fricassee.

Ingredients:

1 kg of egg-plant
125 gms of salted meat or bacon
1 spoonful of ground garlic and ginger
2 finely chopped onions
Thyme, parsley, salt, pepper, ajinomoto
2 tomatoes
Oil

Preparation:

Use the egg-plant called "curry egg-plant", quarter them lengthwise and cut each into 2 so as to have 8 pieces in each egg-plant. (Do not peel the egg-plant). Dice the salted meat or bacon. Mince onions, thyme and parsley.

Cooking:

Pour out two twists of oil in a Chinese wok, put the meat to brown for 1 minute. Add onions, brown 10 seconds, add thyme, parsley, stir and then only add the egg-plant. Put over the vegetable, the ground garlic and ginger. Put on the wooden cover and cook for 2 minutes. Uncover and always in the Chinese fashion (stir fry), that is taking care not to crush the vegetables, place back lid and cook for 2 more minutes, uncover and repeat operation, until the egg-plant are cooked but stay whole.

Chocho Fricassee

Follow the same principles as for the egg-plant fircassee. You must peel the chocho and cut into eight long pieces or else into slices, in which case the cooking will require less time.

Pumpkin Fricassee

After peeling the pumpkin, cut into thin slices as the pumpkin is a vegetable that requires more time for cooking.

Cabbage Fricassee

Pluck out the bigger outer leaves; then cut 2 or 3 of the remaining leaves and proceed in the same way.

Lady Fingers Fricassee

Lady fingers have a particular taste, and contains a sort of glue which gives both a taste and an appearance that can be peculiar. One trick to avoid these inconveniences, take out the supporting stalks with a small knife pierce a hole in the middle of the lady fingers and place them in fire-proof plate in the oven for 5 minutes. You can then proceed to make the fircassee.

The Sponge Gourd Fricassee

Peel and cut the vegetable into dices of 1.5 cms and proceed on the cooking on a very high heat as for the other vegetables.

The Bitter Gourd Fricassee

Halve the gourd and take away the insides with a small spoon. Rub with refined salt, wash in running water and proceed on to the fricassee as usual. The bitter gourd as indicated by its name can have a bitter taste, to which you can remedy by putting 1 spoonful of white sugar during the cooking.

Oysters in Creole Bunn

Ingredients:

2 dozen osyters

150 gms margarine

½ kg of tomatoes

*½ teaspoonful of ground red pepper,
black pepper, salt and ajinomoto*

4 — 6 red peppers

2 small onions

6 round loaves

Preparation:

Shuck the oysters and wash under running water. Drain and scald the tomatoes and peel off. Add black pepper and mince. Slice the bread, take out the crumb and coat the interior with melted margarine and put the bread under the grill for 2 to 4 minutes, so that they can take a golden colour. Keep in a warm place.

Cooking:

Melt the rest of the margarine in a Chinese wok and fry the oysters for 1 minute, take out of the pan and keep warm. Put into the marge, the minced onions and fry for 10 seconds, stir in the red peppers and the ground pepper until brown. Add the minced tomatoes, the ajinomoto, some stock. Simmer for 3 minutes. Stir and then allow some minutes for the sauce to thicken. Put in the oysters cook for another minute, put the sauce into the bunns, sprinkle with bread crumbs and grill for 2 minutes.

Oyster Croquettes

Ingredients:

2 dozen of large shucked oysters

1 cup of self raising flour

1 tablespoonful of white wine

1 tablespoonful of siaw fish sauce

2 tablespoonfuls of starch

¾ cup of water

Oil

2 eggs

Preparation & Frying:

Wash under running cold water the oysters, rub them with salt. Leave for one hour, and wash again.

Place them in a saucepan with water. Bring to a boil, let them boil for 1 minute. Drain and when the oysters are cold enough, marinate in a sauce made of the wine, the siaw sauce and the ajino-moto. Let rest for 1 hour.

Make dough with water, flour, starch and eggs. Put the oysters in the dough. Make some balls and fry in deep oil.

Jellied Eel

Jellied eel is either eaten or drunk by the British around the pubs: it is apparently an excellent remedy when one has a hang over. However it can be a delicious appetizer, served with green salad.

Ingredients:

1 fresh water eel (1½ kg)
2 hard boiled eggs
½ cup of white vinegar
6 pickled olives
2 small pickled gherkins
The juice of a small lemon
2 teaspoonfuls of gelatine (or 1 stick)
Salt and ajinomoto

Preparation & Cooking:

Cut the eel into pieces of 5 cm thick, and soak into vinegar for 20 minutes. Drain and towel dry. Place the pieces in a bowl. Cover with water, to which you will add the lemon juice, salt and ajinomoto. Simmer on a moderate heat for 1 hour; take out the pieces and keep. There must be at least 5 cups of liquid left or else add some water, bring to a boil, dilute the gelatine. Allow to cool. Wash a plate and put in the fridge for 5 minutes. When it is cold, coat it with a thin layer of the gelatine. Decorate with slices of boiled eggs — with minced olives and with slices of gherkins, then put a layer of slices of eel, cover with gelatine and repeat the operation, leave in the fridge for 3 — 4 hours. Run your bowl under tap water, turn your bowl on a bed of lettuce in a large plate.

Fresh Water Shrimps in Tomato Sauce

Ingredients:

1 dozen fresh and large shrimps

½ kg of red tomatoes

3 minced onions

Salt, pepper, ajinomoto, thyme, parsley and bay leaves

Garlic and ginger finely chopped

2 tablespoonfuls of tomato paste

Oil

Preparation:

Put the shrimps in a steamer over high heat until they become red, take them out and scale them. Use the scales to make a paste by grinding them on the grinding slab or electric grinder, mix in the powder thus obtained to two cups of water. Reduce on moderate heat. Drain through a fine sieve or a cheesecloth and keep the juice.

Scald the tomatoes, peel them off and mince.

Cooking:

In a Chinese wok, pour out two twists of oil, when hot stir in the onions until brown. Add garlic and ginger. Stir and brown. Add the tomato paste and minced fresh tomatoes, adding from time to time some of the juice and the rest of the spices. Simmer for 10 minutes. Lastly put in the shrimps and cook for another 15 minutes.

Serve hot with lettuce, slices of boiled eggs and pieces of bread fried in butter.

Fresh Water Shrimps Bitter-Sweet Croquettes

Ingredients:

12 fresh water shrimps

1 egg

1 cup of vinegar and ¾ cup of white sugar

1 tablespoonful of starch

3 garlic pods chopped

6 tomatoes (minced, peeled)

3 finely chopped onions

¼ cabbage

2 carrots

2 tender chochos

1 very small cucumber

1 teaspoonful of red pepper

Lemon juice

Oil

Preparation & Frying:

Cut into thick little sticks all the vegetables. Prepare a frying paste with milk, egg and self-raising flour. Put in the shrimps, make small balls and fry in oil in the Chinese wok. Take out, drain dry and keep warm. In another pan pour out some of the frying oil, heat the oil and brown the garlic for 10 seconds. Then add all the vegetables except the tomatoes. Fry while stirring continuously with a spatula for 30 seconds. Mix in the mixture of sugar and vinegar and the spices (black and red pepper, salt). Bring to a boil. Then add the minced tomatoes. Add some stock (made of the shrimps shells). Simmer until the vegetables are cooked but not mashed. Mix in the starch diluted in some wine. When sauce is thick enough, add the lemon juice and take out. Place the shrimps in a plate and pour over the sauce. Serve hot with rice.

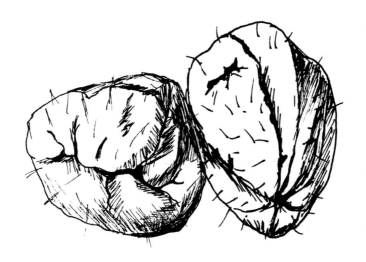

Salted Fish and Bitter Gourd Soup

Ingredients:

250 gms of salted white fish

½ kg of tender bitter gourd

250 gms of tomatoes

1 tablespoonful of minced garlic and ginger

1 teaspoonful of ajinomoto

2 pinch of ground pepper

4 — 6 green pepper cut lengthwise and 1 pinch of red pepper (chillies)

4 minced onions

Boiling water

Oil

Preparation:

This dish apparently simple must be well prepared, and only a Chinese wok should be used.

Soak your fish (cut beforehand into pieces 3 cms thick) in water for ½ hour. Drain. Halve the bitter gourd. Take away the inside. Do not peel the gourd. Soak the gourd in salted water for 15 minutes. Rinse in cold running water and drain.

Scald the tomatoes and mince.

Cooking:

Pour out 2 measures of oil in the Chinese wok. Warm for some seconds and fry the fish to a nice colour; turning frequently. When cooked, take out and keep warm.

Add some more oil, fry the gourd, turning frequently with the spatula. When reduced and yellow, take them out.

Add oil if necessary, brown the onions stirring continuously. Add the garlic and the ginger, the pepper stirring continuously. Put in the fish, turning continuously. Add the minced tomatoes. Brown for 3 minutes until tomatoes are well cooked. Then add the gourd and brown for some more minutes. Add enough boiling water to make a stock. Simmer for 10 minutes. Serve with rice and coconut chutney.

Nerite or Butterfly Shell Soup (Tec-Tec)

The butterfly shell is a small mollusc found in the sand of some beaches of our coast and children find their delight in picking them up. A practical method consists of filling with sand a willow basket and washing out the sand, the nerite remaining at the bottom. One must have at least 3 glasses of butterfly shell.

Ingredients:

3 glasses of butterfly shell

4 — 5 tomatoes

1 tablespoonful of tomato paste

1 tablespoonful of corn flour

1 tablespoonful of chopped garlic
   and ginger

4 — 5 red peppers

2 small chopped onions

Salt and ajinomoto

Chicken stock

Cooking:

Heat the oil in a medium size pan. Brown the onion for 10 seconds. Then add chopped garlic and ginger and the red pepper chopped finely. Add the tomato paste and the chopped tomatoes. Brown for 15 seconds. Dilute in some lukewarm water the cornflour, pour into the pan, stirring continuously. Brown for 2 minutes. Then add the butterfly shell washed thoroughly, simmer until they open up. Add enough boiling water or chicken stock to fill ¾ of the pan, reduce the heat and simmer for 1 hour. Before serving, season to taste with salt and ajinomoto.

The stock is served usually in cups and bowls. If you are patient enough, take out the meat.

Periwinkles are to be found on the sea rocks. The soup is made in exactly the same way.

Vegetables Leave Soup

The leaves of some vegetables have such a nutritive value (iron), that they find a ready place in the Mauritian diet. They are cooked in stock to be served with rice. Very often they attenuate very largely a very spicy curry or rougaille.

Here is a list of leaves commonly used on the island: Drumsticks, watercress, Indian mustard, pumpkins, chochos.

As the leaves can be cooked in very little time, it is preferable to pick the young and tender leaves to have a tastier soup.

Ingredients:

Any leaves of your choice

2 chopped onions

1 tablespoonful of chopped garlic
*   and ginger*

Salt, pepper and ajinomoto

Chicken or beef stock.

Oil

Preparation:

Pick up the leaves, leaving out the strong and hard stalks or stems, wash through clean running water, after soaking them into salted water.

Cooking:

Heat some oil in a medium size pan, brown the pepper then the onions for 10 seconds. Add the chopped garlic and ginger brown for 10 seconds; add the beef or chicken stock, bring to a boil. Add enough water to fill ¾ of the pan. When the water is boiling, throw in the leaves, cover the pan and simmer until the leaves are cooked but do not let them change their colour. Season with salt and ajinomoto to taste. Serve with rice and a rougaille or a curry.

You can easily replace the stock by a piece of meat of chicken or cooked fish, browned before being put into water.

Cassava Catte-Catte (Manioc)

The catte-catte is a typical Creole dish easy to prepare.

Ingredients:

½ kg of good cooking cassava (it may be difficult to find out whether the cassava will be easily cooked or not. One of the easy ways of finding out is to break it, if it breaks easily and it is of white colour, it is the right sort.

250 gms of salted meat diced

Some leaves of drumstick tree

3 — 4 tomatoes finely chopped

3 finely chopped onions

½ teaspoonful of salt and ajinomoto

1 tablespoonful of milk

2 twists of oil

Preparation & Cooking:

Peel the manioc by introducing a sharp knife under the skin and opening it up. Put immediately the cassava in a pan containing fresh water and milk (the milk will prevent the cassava from darkening). Once peeled, cut the cassava layer-wide into pieces of 2 cm and quarter each piece again (thence the name "four-four"). Put right back into the water. In the meantime heat some oil into a pressure cooker. Brown the onions and then the salted meat until it takes a nice colour. Stir in the tomatoes until cooked completely. And then add the manioc that has been drained. Season with salt and ajinomoto. Brown for some minutes then cover with enough water or better still with the meat stock. Put on cover and after the first whistle reduce the heat. Cook for 15 — 20 minutes. Steam off your cooker, open it and pierce with a fork into the cassava if it goes straight in, it is cooked. Add some leaves of drumstick tree. Stew for 2 minutes. Serve hot with a chutney of tomatoes with chillies and pickled lemon.

Jardiniere

This is a meal that is appreciated by all Mauritian. It is traditionally Creole but cooked after the Chinese fashion.

Ingredients:

1 kg of diced beef meat

250 gms of carrots

250 gms of young potatoes

250 gms of tomatoes

1 tin of green peas

1 cauliflower

Salt, pepper, ajinomoto, nutmeg, cloves, Heung New Fun, chopped garlic and ginger

4 chopped onions

1 cup of beef juice

Preparation & Cooking:

Dice the meat, add salt, pepper, nutmeg, cloves and ajinomoto. Heat up some oil in a pressure cooker, brown ginger and garlic and the onions for 10 seconds. Then add the meat and brown for 2 — 3 minutes. Add some juice, cover and steam for 15 minutes. In a Chinese wok, heat up some oil, in it fry carrots with some pepper for 5 minutes. Take them out and keep warm. Then add the potatoes cut into quarters. Leave until they are brown. Take out and keep warm. Fry the cauliflower bunches for some minutes, take out and keep warm too. Pour out some more oil, brown garlic and ginger, add tomatoes and brown. Then add some meat juice, cook for 3 — 4 minutes. Put in the meat, cook for 2 minutes. Then the vegetables; stir without crushing the vegetables by passing the spatula between the vegetables and the pan (stir frying). Add the rest of the meat juice. Stew for another 3 — 4 minutes. Before removing from the heat, add the green peas. The vegetables must be cooked but whole.

Stewed Ox Tail

Ingredients:

1 ox tail cleaned, cut bone by bone

250 gms tender carrots (cut into eight)

250 gms of tomatoes (minced)

Salt, pepper, nutmeg, cloves, cinnamon, ajinomoto, chopped garlic and ginger

125 gms of diced salted meat

1 small glass of cognac (or white wine)

2 onions

Oil

Preparation:

Mix the ox tail with the following spices: salt, garlic, ginger, chopped nutmeg and cloves, thyme and parsley, adjinomoto, cinnamon and leave for ½ hour.

Cooking:

Pour out two twists of oil in the pressure cooker, brown some pepper, then the diced salted meat brown to a nice colour. Then add the carrots and onions. Fry for 5 minutes stirring continuously, add the ox tail, browning for some minutes, then let the tomatoes brown for some minutes. Pour in the wine. Close the cooker and cook for 30 minutes at least. Open and add in the cognac and cook for another 2 minutes.

Serve with rice or bread and lettuce salad.

Carrots/Tomatoes/Sponge Gourd Soup

This soup is very easy to cook. It would be easier if you could use an homogenizer.

Ingredients:

1 kg of sponge gourd or tomatoes or carrots

1 tablespoonful of salt, pepper and ajinomoto

Finely chopped onions

1 bunch of thyme (take away the stalks) and a bunch of chopped parsley.

2 teaspoonfuls of powdered milk

2 white scallions

1 teaspoonful of margarine

Preparation & Cooking:

Cook the vegetables with the following spices: onions, salt, pepper, ajinomoto, thyme, parsley in 1½ litres of water for 20 minutes, (take out the seeds of tomatoes), peel the carrots and cut them into pieces, but do not peel the sponge gourd.

When the vegetables are cooked, drain in a sieve. Mix the liquid part in the homogenizer with the milk powder for 20 seconds. Take out and keep warm. Put in the solid part in the machine and make a paste for 2 — 3 minutes.

Melt your margarine in a pan, brown the scallions, add the paste made of the vegetables. Brown for some minutes. Stir in the milk. Bring to a boil. Stew for 2 — 3 minutes. This soup should be served with pieces of bread fried in margarine. Season to taste.

Stag Legs (Recipe of Ton France)

Ingredients:

4 stag legs washed thoroughly and shaved
(Have the legs sawn at the supermarket
to avoid bruising the bones)

3 glasses of water

Spices:

2 bay leaves

2 Bombay onions

5 whole cloves

2 pieces of nutmeg

3 bunches of spring thyme

6 parsley springs

Salt, pepper and ajinomoto

Slices of beetroot

3 carrots sliced

3 leeks

Lettuce

Some cheese and some flour

Preparation & Cooking:

Boil the stag legs in water with the dry spices on a moderate heat for 2½ hours. Remove from the heat and take out the bones. Boil the vegetables with the thyme for 10 minutes. Grate ¼ of a small tin of cheese, melt 2 tablespoonfuls of margarine in a pan, brown two chopped onions, put in some flour, brown for 10 seconds. Stir in a glass of hot milk to obtain a thick sauce and put in the stag legs. Cook for 2 minutes adding the grated cheese.

In a plate alternate a layer of cooked vegetables and a layer of the stag meat (now in the form of a gelatine).

Serve with mustard.

Stuffed Cabbage

One fine cabbage: when choosing, hold the cabbage in one hand by the stem, beat with the flat of the hand on the cabbage; by the sound you should know whether it is empty or not.

Ingredients for Farced Meat:

1 Bombay onion

4 — 5 tomatoes

125 gms sausage

125 gms minced pork meat

125 gms salted meat or bacon

Thyme, salt, pepper, ajinomoto,
   garlic and ginger

Some oil

Sauce:

1 Bombay onion quartered

4 carrots sliced

1 big potato chopped finely

Some oil

Cooking of the Farced Meat:

Pour out 1 measure of oil, brown the garlic and ginger for 10 seconds. Add the salted meat or diced bacon, brown for 1 minute, remove from heat, keep warm. Put in the minced meat, and the meat of sausages. Cook for 3 — 4 minutes. Remove from oil. Brown in the remaining oil the chopped onion, thyme, parsley and tomatoes. Add the meat and stew on low heat to obtain a consistent farce meat.

Preparation of the Cabbage:

Dip the cabbage into boiling water, to open it up easily; with a small sharp knife take out the heart, fill the cabbage with the farce meat leaf by leaf and of course in the place of the heart. Do not in any case put the meat between the last leaves. Reshape the cabbage again into its natural form and tie it with a piece of string.

Cooking:

Pour out some oil in a large casserole. Brown first the onions, then the carrots and the potatoes; place the cabbage over the vegetables; cover and cook gently for 30 minutes; if necessary add some boiling water. Pour over the sauce on the cabbage from time to time. The cabbage will be cooked when the fork goes straight into the cabbage and is golden.

Cauliflower with the Golden Crest

Ingredients:

1 white cauliflower

125 gms margarine

1 box of bread crumbs

1 bunch of herbs (parsley and thyme)

1 Bombay onion (quartered)

Salt and ajinomoto

1 tablespoonful of powdered milk

Preparation & Cooking:

Cut off the leaves and the stem so that the cauliflower can stay on a plate.

Place in a pan big enough to contain the cauliflower, the herbs, onions, salt, ajinomoto and milk, the cauliflower and water. Bring to a boil and simmer for 20 minutes. If cooked, the knife or fork should go straight. When cooked, take out the cauliflower and place in a round dish. In the meantime, melt in a small casserole or frying pan, the margarine with some ground pepper while stirring continuously. Add in the bread crumbs until you obtain a thick sauce. Pour over the whole cabbage this sauce. Sprinkle with chopped parsley. Surround with lettuce and slices of roasted meat or pork roasted in the Chinese fashion.

Oven Baked Fish

Ingredients:

1 whole fish (1 kg) a capitaine preferably (white fish)

1 teaspoonful of chopped garlic

Salt, pepper, 1 nutmeg, cloves, Heung New Fun and ajinomoto

1 bunch of parsley and thyme

Margarine

Preparation & Cooking:

Scale the fish but do not cut the gills or tail. Remove the entrails. Wash in running water.

Mix all the spices and rub the fish on the interior as well as the exterior. Put some margarine here and there. Put the herbs inside the fish. Place the fish in a large tin foil paper. Foil in and place on the middle rack of the oven and cook for 15 — 20 minutes in moderate heat. Take out and serve in a large plate with a red or white sauce.

Oven Baked Unicorn Fish

Ingredients:

1 big licorn (2 kgs)
2 tablespoonfuls of siaw sauce for fish
2 tablespoonfuls of oil
1 teaspoonful of ajinomoto
1 teaspoonful of "Heung New Fun"
2 Bombay onions
1 bunch of herbs and some pepper
4 — 5 chopped garlic pods

Preparation:

Slit the fish from head to tail. Remove the entrails but do not remove the skin, gills, fins and tail.

Mix the siaw sauce, the oil, ajinomoto, Heung New Fun, chopped onions and the herbs. Mix in the pepper.

Rub the interior of the fish with garlic, put in the faggots and the chopped onions.

Using a big hypodermic syringe with a big bore needle inject some siaw sauce into the fish. Baste the fish with some oil and pepper and place in a grill or the plate of the oven.

Cooking:

Cook for 40 minutes (10 very hot, 20 moderate and 10 again very hot). Serve with a sauce "grand malice" as appetizer or with lettuce salad.

Fish or Octopus Vindaye

The vindaye is one way of cooking the octopus or fish in a spicy vinegar sauce for conservation.

Ingredients:

1 kg of tender octopus or fish

125 gms ginger

125 gms galic

125 gms green saffron diluted into ½ cup of vinegar

6 big red peppers halves

40 cl of mustard oil

250 gms of small onions

Preparation:

Wash the octopus and rub with unrefined salt until the whole glue has disappeared. Pound them on the grinding slab. Cut into pieces. Wash, drain, then mix with table salt and a pinch of ground pepper.

Cooking:

Pour the whole of the oil into the Chinese wok, heat, and fry the octopus. As soon as it becomes red, reduce the heat and cook over a moderate heat for ½ hour. Stir from time to time. Remove from the pan and drain. Brown the garlic and the ginger, add the pepper (and if you like it, add hot red pepper).

Add the crushed green saffron diluted into vinegar and cook for 2 — 3 minutes. Add the small onions, cook for 5 minutes then add the octopus and cook for a few minutes. Sterilize a glassware by boiling it for 15 minutes. Dry and pour your vindaye, which will be nicer if kept for a week or more. Cover your vindaye with hot oil. Each time you serve, use a clean plastic spoon. You can replace the octopus by fried fish. The best fish being the tuna.

You can render the octopus very tender by cooking it in a "slow cooker" for six hours on "minimum" heat.

Fish Vindaye.
Recipe on page 46.

Dry Cod or Salted Shark Meat Au Gratin

The Ministry of Agriculture now has placed on the market shark's meat; after giving it special treatment the meat loses its pungent smell. The meat sold is excellent and is an excellent source of cheap protein. (Can be replaced by dried cod)

Ingredients:

1 kg of salted shark meat or dry cod

½ kg of tomatoes

12 big red peppers

20 cl peanut oil

4 small onions

Garlic and ginger paste

Salt, cayenne pepper, ajinomoto, thyme, parsley and grated nutmeg

Preparation:

Soak the meat or fish for 1 hour into hot water changing the water at least twice. Boil them for ½ hour on a moderate heat. Drain and cut into pieces. Mince the tomatoes, onions, thyme, parsley. Halve the pepper.

Cooking:

Pour out two measures of peanut oil in a Chinese wok, brown the onions for 10 seconds, the tomatoes seasoned with thyme, parsley and nutmeg. Stew for 10 minutes.

Mix the shark's meat with some oil and some cayenne pepper. Coat with margarine a fire proof dish, put in a layer of meat than another of the red sauce, repeat until all ingredients are finished. Pour over rest of oil or melted margarine, sprinkle with bread crumbs and put into a moderate oven for 20 minutes.

The Peperonata

Ingredients:

1 egg per person

Salt, pepper and ajinomoto to taste

½ kg of tomatoes

2 small onions

1 teaspoonful of crushed ginger and garlic

4 twists of oil

Preparation & Cooking:

It is supposed to be an Italian dish but it could also be a Mauritian dish. Prepare a tomato rougaille as indicated elsewhere in a very large frying pan or in a fire proof dish. It will require more oil than an ordinary rougaille. When the sauce is well-cooked, break in an egg (1 per person). Sprinkle with a pinch of pepper and fry until each egg is cooked, pouring frequently over, the oil from the sauce.

Serve with bread or rice or boiled spaghetti.

The Mauriciano Spaghetti

Ingredients:

1 box of 500 gms of spaghetti

½ kg of minced meat with some rashes of bacon

1 tablespoonful of tomato paste

4 — 6 tomatoes

1 small tin of French mushrooms or fresh mushrooms

1 small box of grated cheese (parmesan)

1 tablespoonful of garlic and ginger paste

Salt, pepper and ajinomoto

4 finely chopped onions

Oil

Preparation & Cooking:

Pour out two measures of oil in a pressure cooker, brown some pepper and the minced meat for some minutes. Cover and steam for 10 minutes. Take out the meat, add some more oil if necessary. Brown the garlic, the ginger and the onions; add the tomato paste and the crushed tomatoes. Cook for 3 — 4 minutes. Add the minced meat and bacon. Put some margarine in a frying pan, cook the halved mushrooms and when cooked add it to the meat.

Aslo bring to a boil a large pan of salted water and some oil. When boiling throw in the spaghetti cut into two. Cook for 20 minutes. When cooked, the spaghetti should be crushed easily between the thumb and the finger. Drain the water. Serve in a ring on four plates and pour your meat in the middle.

Serve with grated cheese and Italian wine (chianti).

The Mauritian Risoto

An Italian dish but adapted here and very popular. It can easily be taken on a picnic. The rice cooker makes things so much easier.

Ingredients (for 5):

1 measure of rice per person
½ kg of minced or salted meat
3 small onions
¼ tablespoonful of tomato paste
3 — 4 tomatoes
Salt, pepper and ajinomoto
1 tin of garden peas
Garlic and ginger paste
Grated cheese (parmesan)

Preparation & Cooking:

Pour out two measures of oil in a pressure-cooker, brown the garlic and the ginger, then the minced meat. Cook for 2 minutes. Add 1 table-spoonful of hot water. Close the cooker and cook for 5 minutes.

Remove the meat from the cooker. Add some more oil, brown some pepper, add the tomato paste and crushed tomatoes, add some liquid from the meat. In that red sauce add the meat and cook for 3 minutes. Wash five measures of rice. Put it in the rice cooker with five measures of water, the meat and sauce. After 10 minutes, add the green peas washed thoroughly, and leave until the cooker stops. Serve hot with grated cheese (parmesan).

You can replace the meat with a tin of corned beef cooked directly into the sauce.

Fish Bouillabaisse

Ingredients:

1 fresh fish of 2 kg (capitaine)

1 tablespoonful of saffron

6 tomatoes

2 Bombay onions

1 tablespoonful of ground ginger
  and garlic

2 big chillies

6 fried slices of bread

4 twists of oil

Salt and pepper

Preparation & Cooking:

Scale and clean the fish. Cut it in slices. Rub on the fish slices, saffron, salt and pepper.

Fry the slices of fish in oil. Remove the mid rib and the head of the fish.

In a pressure cooker, brown the onions, ginger and garlic, the chillies, add the head and mid rib of the fish. Add the crushed tomatoes, let it cook for 10 minutes. Add six cups of hot water and cook under pressure for 30 minutes. Remove the pressure. Strain the soup.

In a serving dish, place a slice of fish on a slice of fried bread and pour over it the hot soup.

You can serve this dish in individual bowls.

Mousaka

Ingredients:

1 kg of egg-plant

½ kg of minced meat

150 gms of margarine

4 tomatoes

1 big Bombay onion

2 tablespoonfuls of fresh cream

150 gms of grated cheese

2 eggs

Salt, pepper, ajinomoto and breadcrumbs

Preparation & Cooking:

Slice the egg-plants lengthwise and let the slices soak in salted water.

Brown the slices in melted margarine. In some margarine, brown the onions, add the minced meat, seasoned with salt and pepper. Mix well and cook on mild heat for 30 minutes. Add the crushed tomatoes and cook for a further 10 minutes. Put out the fire and mix in the fresh cream and the uncooked eggs.

In an oven-proof dish alternate layers of egg-plants and cooked meat. Add some cheese and breadcrumbs on top and allow to grate in moderate oven for 15 minutes.

Stuffed Breadfruit

Ingredients:

1 big breadfruit

Rougaille made with 250 gms of either minced meat or minced bacon or minced fish

100 gms of margarine

Preparation & Cooking:

Use a breadfruit that is neither tender nor ripe. With a small carving knife, cut the top head of the fruit and make a hole in the middle. Put the breadfruit in boiling water and cook for 20 minutes. Remove from water and drain. Spread some margarine inside and outside the breadfruit. Stuff the fruit with the rougaille. Cook in a moderate oven for 20 minutes or in a "waterless" pan for 30 minutes.

Potato Soufflé

Ingredients:

1 kg of potatoes

200 gms of grated cheese

2 cups of hot milk

2 eggs

Some nutmeg

Preparation & Cooking:

Peel and cut the potatoes in slices. Beat the 2 eggs in an omelette form and add the nutmeg.

In an oven-ware (with a high rim), alternate one layer of potato and one layer of cheese. Whisk the eggs and the milk and pour it over the potatoes and cook in a moderate oven for 40 minutes.

Grilled Fish

Ingredients:

1 kg of fresh fish (Bourgeois, Carangue,
   Vieille rouge)

Salt, pepper, ajinomoto, thyme, parsley
   green chillies, mint and coriander leaves

The juice of 3 lemons

2 tablespoonfuls of olive oil

6 tomatoes

Preparation & Cooking:

Clean and scale the fish, make some small cuts in the flesh. Pour over the fish, the lemon juice and let maninate for 1 hour.

Cut the green spices in small pieces, mix it with salt, pepper and ajinomoto. Rub the fish with this mixture. Pre-heat the grill and grill the fish for 20 minutes on each side.

Just before serving, cut the tomatoes in slices and place them over the fish and let grill for a further 10 minutes. Add the rest of the lemon juice and serve on a bed of lettuce.

Octopus Daube in Coconut Juice

Ingredients:

1 kg of young octopus

2 onions

1 bunch of thyme

1 tablespoonful of pounded ginger
   and garlic

1 cup of coconut juice

Salt, pepper and ajinomoto

Preparation of Coconut Juice:

Grate the coconut finely, put the coconut in a piece of muslin cloth, and squeeze the juice. You can use a juice extractor instead.

Preparation and Cooking:

Wash the octopus with kitchen salt and put it in a casserole with very little water, and let it cook very slowly for 1 hour. (You can also use a "slow cooker" for six hours.) Remove the octopus, slice it and save the juice.

In very little oil, brown the onion, garlic paste and thyme, add the sliced octopus and the coconut juice gradually and cook for a further 10 minutes.

Grated Potatoes or Yam with Dried Cod

Ingredients:

1 kg of potatoes or yam
250 gms of dried cod
1 cup of milk
2 tablespoonfuls of margarine
2 small onions
1 teaspoonful pounded ginger and garlic
1 bundle of thyme
2 eggs
Some breadcrumbs

Preparation and Cooking:

Soak the dried cod in water for 1 hour. Cut the potatoes in small pieces. Boil the cod and potatoes or yam in a pressure cooker for 20 minutes. Drain and crush the mixture with a big fork.

In a Chinese wok, melt some margarine and brown the onions, thyme, and garlic paste. Add the mixture of cod and potatoes, mix well by gradually adding the milk. Put out the fire and mix in the 2 eggs.

Spread some margarine in an oven-proof dish and pour in the mixture. Spread some breadcrumbs and grate in a moderate oven for 15 minutes.

Stir Fried Cho-Cho and Salted Fish

Ingredients:

1 kg of very tender cho-cho
250 gms of salted fish
2 big onions
4 big chillies
*1 tablespoonful pounded ginger
  and garlic*
The juice of 2 lemons
2 twists of oil

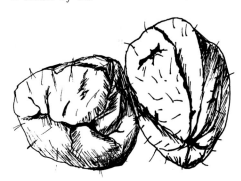

Preparation:

Peel the cho-cho and grate it. Slice the onions. Allow the salted fish to remain in cold water for 1 hour, drain and cut in small pieces. Slice the chillies.

Cooking:

In a big Chinese wok pour 2 twists of oil. Fry the salted fish for 5 minutes. Remove and keep warm. Brown the onions, chillies and ginger paste and add the cho-cho. Stir fry the cho-cho, add the fish, mix well and just before serving add the lemon juice.

Serve with rice and dholl or lentils.

Chicken Liver Paté

Ingredients:

½ kg of chicken livers
1 tin of fresh cream
2 small onions
3 twigs of thyme
1 tablespoonful of brandy
1 tablespoonful of margarine
Salt and pepper

Preparation & Cooking:

In a small wok brown the onions and thyme in some margarine. Add the chicken livers mix well and cook for 15 minutes.

Put the lot in a mixer add the fresh cream, mix for a few minutes and then add the brandy. Mix again. Allow to cool in the refrigerator.

Serve on small toasts.

Chicken cooked in Peanut Butter

Ingredients:

1 chicken of 1 kg
1 big onion
6 tomatoes
1 tablespoonful of peanut butter
200 gms of roasted peanut
1 twist of oil
Salt, pepper and ajinomoto

Preparation:

Cut the chicken in pieces, slice the onion and crush the roasted peanut.

Cooking:

Put a twist of oil in a Chinese wok. Brown the onions, add the peanut butter and a tablespoonful of warm water, mix well, add the pieces of chicken. Cover and allow to cook for 10 minutes. Uncover and add the crushed tomatoes and cook for a further 10 minutes. Just before serving add the crushed roasted peanuts.

Chicken cooked with Pineapple

Ingredients:

1 chicken of 1 kg

1 big pinapple

3 Bombay onions

6 tomatoes

Some cloves and cinnamon

125 ml of red wine

1 twist of oil

100 gms of margarine

Salt, pepper and ajinomoto

Preparation & Cooking:

Cut the chicken in small pieces. Mix with salt pepper and ajinomoto.

Peel the pineapple and cut in slices. Homogenise into a paste using a blender, 2 slices of pineapple, the tomatoes and the red wine.

In a casserole brown the onions, cloves and cinnamon. Add the chicken pieces. Brown them on all sides, and cook for 20 minutes, remove and keep warm.

In the remaining sauce add the tomatoes and pineapple mixture and cook for 10 minutes. Fry the remaining slices of pineapple in some margarine.

Put the cooked chicken in a plate. Cover with the sauce and decorate with the pineapple slices.

CHINESE CUISINE

Squid and Cauliflower.
Recipe on page 65.

The Chinese Sauces

The Chinese have hundreds of little sauces to accommodate the different dishes.

Mustard Oil Garlic Sauce

Chop finely some garlic pods, put in low fire-proof dish. Heat some mustard oil in a Chinese wok until it starts smoking. Pour this oil over the chopped garlic and season to taste. Add siaw sauce and mix well.

Garlic Sauce

Widely used. Serves very well with croquettes, Chinese sausages, roasted meat, hakien etc.

5 shelled garlic pods, chopped on the Chinese chopping log mixed with salt into a consistent paste. Dilute with hot white vinegar. Add some salt and chopped scallions.

Mustard Sauce

Dilute 2 tablespoonfuls of mustard in boiling water, mix into a consistent paste. Add a tablespoonful of vinegar, some salt, cool down to room temperature, add olive oil, whisk like a mayonnaise.

Pepper Sauce

125 gms of green pepper, some garlic, ⅔ ginger pods. Grind everything on a slab. Dilute into a bowl, 2 spoonfuls of olive oil, 1 spoonful of white rhum, some salt, some white pepper, 2 spoonfuls of vinegar, mix and serve with a clean spoon.

This sauce keeps very well in a sterilized jar.

Crab Soup

The crab soup is one of the first Chinese dishes to "invade" the other Mauritian kitchens. It is supposed to be an aphrodisiac and very good after having a hang-over. It started the fame of Gros Piti, the great hotel where the whole high society would go to eat after the races in Port Louis.

Ingredients:

2 large live crabs
1 tablespoonful of starch
6 red tomatoes
1 bunch of chopped thyme
Some minced onions
4 big chopped peppers
1 pinch of red chillie
1 teaspoonful of ajinomoto
1 bunch of scallion
Some oil and some chicken stock

Preparation & Cooking:

Kill the 2 large crabs in the Chinese fashion, that is by forcing a knife into the apron. Clean them and keep only the white parts. Throw away the fat.

Pour one twist of oil in a Chinese wok, brown some minced onions, 1 spoonful of starch, stir for 4 seconds, add the thyme and the tomatoes. Add the uncooked crabs. Stir until the meat becomes slightly red. Add the minced chillies and red pepper, and almost at the same time, the chicken bone stock (hot), stew for 20 minutes on a very mild heat. Right before removing, add 1 spoonful of ajinomoto and 1 bunch of scallion.

The soup must be served very hot in Chinese bowls and Chinese spoons which makes it possible to drink it hot.

Fish Ball or Van-Yen Soup

This soup is the same one you can see being sold at the Chinese hotels in Port Louis. It can easily be cooked at home, but I would advise to buy the fish balls already made. They can keep very well in the fridge.

Ingredients:

½ kg of pork legs

2 — 3 fish heads

1 measure of small periwinkles

1 teaspoonful of salt

1 teaspoonful of ajinomoto

1 bowl of cooked rice

1 small cup of milk

1 small faggot of herbs and chopped scallions

8 — 10 fish balls per person.

Preparation & Cooking:

Boil in a pressure cooker on a moderate heat, for 2 hours at least, the following ingredients: the pork legs, the fish heads, the periwinkles, salt, ajinomoto, the faggot and 10 bowls of cold water. In the meantime, homogenise the milk and the rice to have a white homogenous liquid. Then drain in the sieve. Keep the liquid.

Warm some oil in a pan, brown the scallions, add the milk and rice, stirring continuously. Add gradually your stock, boil for some minutes. Put in the van-yen and cook for 5 minutes. Take them out and serve as soon as the balls start expanding. Serve hot with Chinese spoons. The pork legs can be served with a vinegrette sauce as appetizer.

Mee Foon Soup and Special Noodles (Yee Mein)

Ingredients:

½ kg of Chinese noodles or Yee Mein

Chicken bones or ½ kg of chicken legs

½ tin of bamboo shoots

10 — 12 Chinese mushrooms "Tong-Ku"

Chicken meat cut into pieces

*Some shrimps and rest of crabs/fish
    or lobster*

Ajinomoto, salt, pepper and siaw

2 teaspoonfuls of corn flour or maizena

3 finely chopped onions

Preparation:

Hack into pieces the chicken bones. Warm some oil in a pressure cooker. Add some pepper and 3 finely chopped onions. Then add the hacked bones, brown for 3 — 4 minutes. Add then 6 bowls of warm water, cover and cook for about 1 hour from the first whistle.

In the meantime, add to the chicken the cornflour, 1 spoonful of ajinomoto, some pepper, mix and let soak for 15 minutes. Wash the bamboo shoots and the mushrooms, scale the shrimps and chop the lobster or crab meat.

Cooking:

Pour out 2 measures of oil in a great Chinese wok. Fry the mushrooms for 3 — 5 minutes, remove and keep warm, put in the bamboo shoots, fry for 5 minutes. Stirring continuously, remove and keep warm.

Add some more oil, if necessary fry the shrimps, the crab and the lobster and then the chicken. When the chicken is cooked after 5 — 8 minutes, add the crab, lobster, shrimp and mushrooms, bamboo shoots. Mix well and cook for another 2 minutes. Put stock into a large pan and bring to boil. Put in the noodles (1 portion per person) and cook for 3 — 4 minutes. When cooked, the noodles should easily be crushed.

Pour out into individual Chinese bowls and then put in the meat. By itself it is a complete dish and if you wish to make the real treat put in an egg fried in butter (one egg per person).

Toong Foon or Mee Foon Soup

Ingredients:

Chicken bones
½ kg of Mee foon or Toong foon
1 teaspoonful of salt and ajinomoto
Some leaves of pickled Chinese cabbages
Some chicken meat
1 teaspoonful of rice alcohol (chaw sui)
Oil

Preparation & Cooking:

Hack into small pieces the chicken bones, boil in 7 bowls of water for 2 hours on a medium heat.

Warm some oil in a Chinese wok, brown the chicken for some minutes with salt, add the stock, bring to a boil, add the rice alcohol and the Mee Foon. Reduce the heat and stew for 10 minutes. Add the pickled Chinese cabbage, ajinomoto and remove from heat.

Serve in little bowls with a Chinese spoon.

Kai-Chock or Mama Soup

This soup is a very popular Chinese dish owing to a small Chinese restaurant that bore that name during the 60's.

Ingredients:

½ kg of fish fillet
5 bowls of stock (made out of fish head)
250 gms of rice
1 teaspoonful of brandy
1 piece of chopped ginger
Some olive oil
Salt, ajinomoto and siaw
1 fried egg per person

Preparation:

Place the fish on the slab and hack with 2 knives. Mix in salt and ajinomoto. Wash the rice and chop scallions. Take half of the fish, mix with oil, ginger, brandy and siaw.

Cooking:

Take the first half of fish and boil it in the stock with the rice for 30 minutes in a pressure cooker on a low heat. Uncover and cook some more minutes until a thick mash. Then add the rest of the raw fish, mix and bring to a boil.

Serve immediately in Chinese bowls, put in the chopped scallions and decorate with fried eggs and some olive oil.

Roasted Eggs in the Chinese Fashion

The roasted eggs are those succulent eggs that you find in Chinese restaurants, they are excellent appetizers. The recipe I am going to give you equals the price you have paid for this book, for it is at the cost of a long battle, and many resorts to subterfuge, that I succeeded in obtaining the real recipe.

Ingredients:

It would be more economical to make 24 eggs as the ingredients are rather expensive.

24 fresh eggs

40 cl of red wine (cheap wine)

20 cl of siaw sauce for meat

1 glass of water and same amount of oil

1 tablespoonful of red rice or "siouk"

1 tablespoonful of Heung New Fun or five spices

1 tablespoonful of Chinese anis (wrapped in a fine cheesecloth)

Preparation & Cooking:

Put all the eggs in a large pan of cold water, bring to a boil and boil for 15 — 30 minutes, until they are really hard boiled.

In another casserole, mix all the other ingredients and add the shelled eggs. Bring to a boil and cook for some time on a moderate heat. The eggs will be roasted when all the water will have evaporated.

Keep the sauce. Put the sauce in the fridge and if some is left for the next day, warm in the sauce to stop from desintegrating. You can serve the same sauce for some days but you should keep it in the fridge.

If the eggs are too salted, add some white sugar to the sauce, serve the eggs cut into four with garlic sauce.

Squid and Cauliflower

This is a Chinese recipe that needs a few minutes cooking and that is served with rice or bread.

Ingredients:

1 kg of tender squid

1 whole cauliflower

1 tablespoonful of siaw sauce for fish

1 tablespoonful of starch

Some chopped garlic pods, 1 piece of chopped ginger, salt, pepper, ajinomoto and a chopped onion

2 small Bombay onions

Preparation:

Clean and cut into small pieces the squid. If you have enough time, you could trim into flower shapes or lace fashion; this will not change the taste of course, but will give a more pleasant appearance. Soak the squid into boiling water and drain, on the other hand, break the cauliflower bunches, taking care not to put the stems that can be hard.

Cooking:

Pour out 1 measure of oil in a Chinese wok, brown the chopped onion, the ginger. Stir in the squid; put a wooden lid and cook for 5 minutes.

Dissolve the starch in some water, stir into the wok, add the siaw sauce and the ajinomoto. When the squid is cooked, add the cauliflower. Stir continuously on a very high heat for 3 minutes. Then add the Bombay onions, cook for another 2 minutes.

It is necessary to cook under a fierce heat. The cauliflower must remain whole but cooked. Serve with rice and tomato chutney.

Fish and Sponge Gourd

Ingredients:

½ kg of fillet fish

1 kg of sponge gourd

1 tablespoonful of siaw sauce for fish

Some salt, pepper, ajinomoto and some corn flour

Chopped garlic (3 pods)

1 small piece of ginger

1 large Bombay onion (cut into eight)

3 tablespoonfuls of white wine

Oil

Preparation:

Slice the fillets into flat pieces; put them in a bowl, mix with corn flour, pepper, ajinomoto and leave for 15 minutes.

Peel the gourds, take away the interior and cut into pieces, wash and drain.

Mix together the cornflour, the siaw, the white wine.

Cooking:

Pour out 2 measures of oil in a Chinese wok. Brown the garlic and the ginger. Then put in the fish and cook for 5 minutes. Make a well in the middle of the ingredients and pour the sauce mixture. As soon as the sauce starts thickening, mix well in all the ash gourd, stir fry for 3 more minutes.

Serve with rice and tomato and coriander chutney.

Son Thi Ham Fish

Ingredients:

1 kg of fish fillet

½ glass of white vinegar

1 tablespoonful of white sugar

1 pickled lemon

1 teaspoonful of cornflour

Some red chopped pepper, ajinomoto and salt

Oil

Preparation:

Cut into slices 1 cm × 1 cm × 4, the fillets. Add some pepper and some cornflour. Mix well. Prepare a sauce with white sugar, vinegar, red pepper, ajinomoto and the lemon (reduced into a paste).

Cooking:

Pour 4 measures of oil into the Chinese wok. Fry the fish, stirring continuously for 30 seconds, put a wooden lid and cook for 10 seconds. Uncover, stir and cover again for another 30 seconds. Uncover and add the sauce, mix and cook on a very high heat. Use the spatula to prevent the sauce from coating the sides of the wok. Serve with rice.

The Sweet and Sour Fish

The sweet and sour fish is one of those mysterious dishes that are however very easy to make. It constitutes an excellent and pleasant to sight hors d'oeuvre. Serve with a well-chilled rosé wine.

It is preferable to boil the fish in the Chinese fashion, that is whole and for that a large pan is used.

Ingredients:

1 large fish of 1 kg (damberri)

1 young cucumber

2 small tender carrots

2 small green and young chocho

1 big piece of ginger

2 spoonfuls of white sugar

½ cup of white vinegar

2 spoonfuls of starch

1 teaspoonful of ajinomoto, salt and pepper

1 Bombay onion

Oil

Preparation:

Peel the carrots, chocho, cucumber and the ginger. Slice them into small sticks 2 cm long. Chop a Bombay onion. Place all the vegetables in one bowl, mix well and put in 1 spoonful of salt. Leave for 10 minutes. Then add 2 spoonfuls of sugar, ½ cup of vinegar and ½ cup of water. Let the fish marinate in this for ¾ hour.

Cooking:

Boil some water in the fish pan and add 2 spoonfuls of salt, 2 spoonfuls of oil. Bring to a boil again, put in the fish. Cover and stop the heat. Let the fish cook in the water temperature for ½ hour.

Drain the vegetables and put them in a bowl. Make a sauce out of the marinade, add sugar if you want. Dissolve the starch into water. Heat some oil in a pan, add 2 garlic pods finely chopped; put in dissolved starch, stir continuously and add from time to time the marinade sauce and the ajinomoto. Let the sauce thicken. Stir in the vegetables and stir fry for 20 — 30 seconds only.

Place the fish in a plate, warm it up if necessary. Cover with your sauce and the vegetables. You can decorate with some mee-foon fried in oil for some minutes. Decorate with lettuce, slices of tomatoes.

Some people prefer to eat fried fish with this sauce. Fry the fish fillets, place them in a plate and pour over the sauce (made from the oil of the fried fish).

Sweet and Sour Squid

Ingredients:

1 kg of squid
3 young cucumbers
3 small carrots
½ cup of vinegar
2 tablespoonfuls of water
3 tablespoonfuls of white sugar
2 tablespoonfuls of corn flour
1 spoonful of siaw sauce for fish
2 garlic pods
1 piece of chopped ginger
Salt, pepper and ajinomoto
Oil

Preparation of the Vegetables:

Cut the carrots and cucumber into match sticks, place them into a plate, sprinkle with salt and let for 10 minutes, then add sugar, water and vinegar. Blend well and let it marinate for 30 minutes.

Drain the vegetables and keep the juice. Add to it the siaw, the corn flour and some salt.

Cut the squid into pieces in the Chinese fashion. Put into scalding water for 2 minutes.

Cooking:

Pour out 2 measures of oil in a Chinese wok, brown the garlic and the ginger finely chopped; put in the squid to which you will have added some pepper. Brown and cover with a wooden lid. Stew for 5 minutes. Uncover and make a well in the middle. Pour in the marinate sauce. Allow to thicken, then mix briskly with a spatula. Stir in the vegetables and stir fry. If necessary add some hot water, cover and simmer for 3 — 4 minutes. The squid must be well cooked and the vegetables firm to make a success of this dish.

Serve as a hors d'oeuvre with lettuce and bread.

Mauritian Method
of Preserving
Spices, Condiments etc.

Young Chicken Boiled in the Chinese Fashion

The chicken cooked in this way is recommended to those who cannot eat too spicy meals and to convalescent people and small children.

Ingredients:

1 young fat chicken or very young capon
2 tablespoonfuls of olive oil
Salt and pepper
Freshly prepared mustard cream

Preparation:

Choose a young fat chicken or a very young capon. The fowls must be tender as a very short time of cooking is the secret of this recipe. Plunge the bird into scalding water to make the plucking easier. The Chinese proceed this way: starting from the beak, press towards the root, this method has the advantages of leaving a minimum of feathers and avoiding harming the meat.

When the chicken is clean, make a round incision round the anus and straight cut near the crop. Through the opening pull out the wind pipe and the oesophagus and then by the other opening pull out the whole digestive organ.

Fold the legs without breaking them and insert within the belly. The chicken is now ready to be cooked in a pan large enough to contain it.

Cooking:

Place the pan filled with water and the chicken on the belly on a moderate heat. Bring to a boil. Then with a long fork, take out the chicken and drip dry for a few seconds. (This is important for the water inside the chicken is less hot than the water on the outside and it is important that the chicken should be cooked both sides). When the water on the inside is drained, put back the chicken, on the back this time, into the water. Boil for 5 minutes and repeat the operation. Put back the chicken, first on the left then on the right side and lastly, back on the belly. Leave for 5 minutes and remove from the water. Place in a plate until you can hold the chicken by the hand. Rub with table salt and let it cool down.

When completely cold, then only proceed to cut the meat into small pieces (meat and bone except for the sides and legs).

Arrange in a plate, reshaping as much as possible the chicken. Pour over 2 spoonfuls of olive oil and serve with a mustard sauce and garlic.

Chicken and Garden Peas

Ingredients:

1 small chicken of 1 kg
1 tin of garden peas
4 — 5 tomatoes
6 onions
Salt, pepper and ajinomoto

Preparation:

Pluck and clean the chicken. Cut with a Chinese knife into small pieces. Chop finely the onions and wash in a colander.

Cooking:

Pour out 4 measures of oil in a Chinese wok. Brown the chicken for 2 minutes stirring continuously. Cook the onions. Mix well. After 3 minutes, add boiling water to fill ½ of the pan Cover with a wooden lid and stew for 3 minutes. Add the tomatoes passed through the homogenizer, mix, cover and cook for 5 minutes. You can turn the pieces one more time. Add some hot water and the garden peas. Cook for 3 minutes.

Serve with rice or bread.

Three Marvel Chicken or Shamtung Chicken

Ingredients:

1 small chicken of 1 kg
10 "Tong Ku" mushrooms
1 bunch of ear mushrooms
1 tin of bamboo shoots
8 chopped onions
Oil

Spices:

2 pinch of salt
2 spoonfuls of starch
1 tablespoonful of siaw sauce

Spices for Sauce:

4 tablespoonfuls of red wine
2 pinches of starch
1 teaspoonful of ajinomoto

Preparation for the Meat:

Bone the chicken, and cut the meat into thin strips, add the gizzard (cut into a flower form) and the liver. Mix with the salt, siaw, starch and keep.

Preparation of the Vegetables:

Cut the bamboo shoots into sticks or lace like in the Chinese fashion and put into a bowl. The onions, the mushrooms are to be placed in separate bowls.

Cooking:

On a very high heat, pour 1 measure of oil in a Chinese wok and when the oil is hot, fry the bamboo shoots for 6 — 10 seconds. Remove from heat and keep warm.

Add some more oil, brown in the same way, the different mushrooms, stirring continuously for 60 seconds. Then add the bamboo shoots, mix briskly once or twice. Remove and keep warm.

Add some more oil, fry the meat while stirring for 80 seconds, add the onions, bamboo shoots and the mushrooms. Put a wooden lid, cook for 2 minutes.

In the meantime, prepare a mixture of the red wine and starch, add to the meat, turn for 2 or 3 times. Remove from heat.

Serve hot with rice and tomato chutney.

Chicken with Large Green Peppers

Ingredients:

1 chicken of 1 kg
3 Jamaica peppers, cut lengthwise
3 tablespoonfuls of siaw
1 tablespoonful of starch
Salt, pepper and ajinomoto
4 tablespoonfuls of red wine
Oil

Preparation:

Bone the chicken, and cut the meat into pieces, add siaw sauce, and some starch. Prepare a sauce with wine, the rest of the starch, some siaw and ajinomoto.

Cooking:

Heat in a Chinese wok 2 measures of oil. Fry the Jamaica peppers with salt for 20 seconds. Remove and keep warm. Fry the meat for 2 minutes, add the peppers and the sauce. Stir and cook for 1 minute.

Bitter Gourd, Chicken Liver and Gizzard

Ingredients:

6 green bitter gourds
250 gms of mixed liver and gizzard
1 teaspoonful of sugar
4 garlic pods chopped
Salt, pepper and ajinomoto
1 tablespoonful of starch dissolved in
    red wine
1 chopped piece of ginger
Oil

Preparation:

Halve the gourds, clean the interior and slice. Cut into two the liver and into four the gizzard, put them into a plate with pepper, starch and ajinomoto.

Cooking:

Pour out 1 measure of oil in a Chinese wok. On a high fire, fry the garlic and ginger. Stir in the gourds, add the siaw sauce, the sugar and fry for 1½ minutes. Remove from heat and keep warm.

Fry on high heat the liver and gizzard in the wok for 3 — 5 minutes; while frying, pour in the starch dissolved in the wine, stirring constantly. Put back the gourds and cook for another minute.

Serve hot with rice.

Chicken Croquettes

Ingredients:

½ of a chicken of 1½ kg
  (for 25 — 30 croquettes)

350 gms of flour

1 teaspoonful of baking powder

¾ tablespoonful of salt

¾ small measure of peanut oil

1 teaspoonful of ajinomoto

1 tablespoonful of siaw sauce

3 pinches of ground pepper

15 ml of white rhum

Oil

Preparation of the Meat:

Take out from the chicken the liver and the gizzard. Cut into two the chicken, bone the half in such a way that the meat stays whole. Cut into strips this meat of 6 — 8 cm long and 3 — 6 cm wide. Add a spoonful of siaw sauce, pepper and rhum, blend well and keep in a plate.

Preparation for the Dough:

Put 250 gms of flour in a bowl. Dissolve ¾ spoonful of salt into ½ cup of water. Mix into the flour, 1 spoonful of baking powder, ⅔ measure of peanut oil, salted water, whisk and knead in cold water until the flour becomes a firm paste but not hard. The paste must be homogenous, add a spoonful of ajinomoto and stir.

Cooking:

Place on a moderate heat, a Chinese wok in which you will have poured 1 litre of oil (the croquettes must float in the oil). When the oil is very hot, take one by one the strips of meat, put them in the dough so as to have a ball and throw in the oil. Do not put too many balls together so that they do not stick. Separate them, from time to time with a thin iron rod, fry until they have a nice colour. At that point, remove and drain in a "chaw leo" or a Chinese basket.

Serve hot in a round plate. In the middle, place a small bowl with garlic sauce.

Mee Foon

Mee foon means in hacca rice vermicelli. It is sold in packets of 1 lb (nearly 450 gms). In 1 packet there are four layers, one of which constitute one portion.

Ingredients:

1 packet of mee foon
1 young chicken
1 small bunch of scallion
4 eggs
1 teaspoonful of ajinomoto
1 teaspoonful of corn flour (starch)
Oil and siaw

Preparation:

Cut the scallion into pieces of 2 cm long. Break the eggs in a bowl. Bone the chicken and cut the meat into strips of 4 cm, cut the gizzard into small squares.

Add 1 spoonful of starch and mix.

Cooking:

(It is important to keep the timing in the different steps).

Put the mee foon into boiling water for 5 minutes until cooked. Remove when cooked and drain in a Chinese basket. (Let it cool off for 3 hours)

Pour out in a Chinese wok, 2 measures of oil and heat. Add to the chicken, some pepper, salt and siaw sauce, blend and fry immediately.

When the oil is very hot:

Timing in seconds:

0°	Fry the chicken without stirring for 30 — 40 seconds. Then stir from time to time, bringing the pieces to the sides of the wok.
105°	After 1 minute 45 seconds, remove and place in a bowl.
0°	Put the cold mee foon in the wok in the oil in which the chicken has been fried. Salt with siaw sauce. Break, turn and lift the mee foon with 2 Chinese sticks or a big fork.
60°	Add the eggs and mix.
90°	Add the chicken and 1 spoonful of ajino-moto and blend.
120°	Add the scallions, mix and cook for 45 seconds.

Serve immediately with some siaw sauce, garlic sauce and a tomato chutney.

Chinese Beefsteak

The beefsteak or fried meat is a main meal easy to cook but so badly prepared, in some Mauritian families. With a minimum preparation and some common sense, the meat can be fried deliciously. But the secret lies probably in the choice of good meat, for the Chinese cooking requires very little time, in order to keep all the nutritive value and taste.

Ingredients:

1 kg of beef fillets
3 sweet biscuits
1 tablespoonful of starch (corn flour)
2 tablespoonfuls of sweet condensed milk
2 tablespoonfuls of siaw sauce
1 teaspoonful of ground pepper

Preparation:

Cut with the grain into thin slices the veal or fillet, take out all the fat (strings, nerves). Beat the meat on the chopping log with the knife handle or with the meat hammer.

Crush the biscuits. Mix the starch, the pepper. Flatten the prepared meat in a plate. Spray on a thin layer of condensed milk and the siaw. Sprinkle the mixture of biscuits, starch and pepper. Blend well to have an homogenous surface.

Cooking:

Warm the oil in the wok. When warm, place the pieces one by one. Fry on the first side (count 1 — 18 normally) and fry the same way the other side. Then fry on the first side (counting 1 — 4) repeat for the other side. Arrange in a plate and serve hot. You can then pour out 1 spoonful of siaw sauce, the siaw replacing the salt.

Fried Rice or Cantonnese Rice

Fried rice is one of those Chinese meals so easily prepared that it has been adopted largely by the other sections of the population.

Ingredients (for 1 person):

200 gms of uncooked rice or 1 rice cooker measure of rice

50 gms of Chinese sausages

1 egg

2 spoonfuls of chopped scallion, siaw sauce and oil or dripping 5 cl of white wine

You can also add remains of beef meat, or chicken or sausage meat or even fried fish cut into pieces.

Preparation for the rice:

To be a success, the rice must be tender but firm. The best device to cook the rice is to use the Japanese rice cooker, a remarkable apparatus that enables anyone to cook the rice the different ways. But it is necessary to put the right proportion of water. Usually calculate one measure less of water for the rice than for the ordinary cooking i.e. 3 measurs of rice = 5 measures of water, 6 measures of rice = 10 measures of water. (Allow the rice to cool for 2 hours)

Preparation:

Slice thinly the sausages. Mince the meat (chicken or beef), chop the scallions and whisk the eggs as for an omelette.

Pour out 2 measures of oil in a Chinese wok.

Stir in the sausages for 60 — 90 seconds, remove from heat and keep warm.

Then stir in the meat with 1 spoonful of ajino-moto and cook for 3 — 5 minutes. Remove and keep warm.

For the eggs: two methods — (1) put the egg whisked straight into the wok and whisk briskly to have as many wisps of eggs as possible. Cook for a few seconds only. (2) Make a traditional omelette in a frying pan and then cut into thin strips (Julienne).

Use half of the omelette to put into the rice and half to decorate.

Cooking:

Now, add some more oil into the wok, heat and pour in your cold rice, brown the rice for 60 seconds. Then add the sausages, meat and eggs. Cook for 2 minutes stirring continuously. Then add the siaw sauce until a nice colour. When the rice have been cooked for 3 minutes, put in the chopped scallions and white wine, mix and remove from the heat after 1 minute.

Serve hot with a nice hot tomato chutney.

Chinese Sausages

The Chinese sausages served as appetizers or mixed with fried rice, or the fried mee-foon or even in a tomato Creole sauce, are very popular. Use ¾ lean and ¼ fat pork.

Ingredients:

½ kg of meat

10 gms of salt

10 gms of sugar

20 ml of rhum

2 gms of salpetre and small intestine of pork or artificial lining

Preparation of the Meat:

You will need a meat hammer and a sausage filler.

Buy, fresh and long tripes from the butcher, wash them in clean water after scraping them with the back of a spoon. This scraping removes the mucous membrane leaving the thin envelope. When the mucous membrane has been expelled. completely, wash the interior by adapting one side to the tap and allowing the water to run for a length of time.

Take away the bones and the skin, cut the meat into strips of 3 — 5 cm long and ½ cm large. Mix in the meat, the spices mentioned above in the indicated proportions.

Force the meat into the tripes.

The Making of Sausages:

Use a mincer adapted with a sausage filler. Place on the filler, a large piece of tripe. Squeeze tight one end of the tripe. Use a cork pierced through by a dozen of pins, to pierce the sausage film as soon as the sausage is formed. This is necessary to enable the air to get out of the sausage as well as the water oozing from the meat. Place the meat into the mincer and start turning the handle. The meat should go straight into the film prepared. Press gently on the tripe at the required length and you will have automatically one sausage. Pierce through, each air bulb that will appear in the sausage, and pierce the sausage all through. Tie the end with a string. Hang up the sausage for 3 — 4 days, exposed to the sun and air.

To serve as appetizer, slice, cook in warm oil for 10 — 15 seconds, or steam for 15 minutes and serve with a hot pepper garlic sauce.

Lobster or Crab Foo-Yung

The Foo-Yung is a sort of Chinese omelette in which lobster or crab is woven in.

Ingredients:

50 gms of Chinese mushrooms (Tong Ku)

6 eggs

Meat from 2 crabs or 1 lobster cut into pieces

6 onions and 1 small carrot cut into sticks

1 bunch of soya beans sprouts

3 small onions

2 tablespoonfuls of siaw sauce

Salt, pepper and ajinomoto

1 tablespoonful of starch (corn flour)

½ tablespoonful of white sugar

25 ml of white rhum

Preparation:

Soak the mushrooms and take away the supporting stalks and cut into thin pieces.

Whisk the eggs (white and yolks).

Mix in the eggs to the crab meat, rhum, soya beans, 1 spoonful of siaw, the chopped onions.

Cooking:

Pour out 4 measures of oil in a Chinese wok; put 1 spoonful of the mixture into the oil and fry on all sides. Fry all the whole mixture in this way.

Make a sauce with the starch, the siaw, the sugar, pepper and ajinomoto; thicken on heat for some minutes. Turn over this sauce over the warm Foo-Yung and serve immediately.

Crab Fancy Cakes (Hakien)

Ingredients:

2 large crabs

½ kg of roasted fresh pork

1 bunch of Chinese garlic

⅓ tin of bamboo shoots

1 bunch of "Tong Ku" and 2 of (Chinese) mushrooms

75 cl of oil

Preparation:

Kill the crabs in the Chinese way. Steam it this way. Place the meat on a fire-proof plate, boil some water in a very large pan and as soon as the water starts boiling, put in an empty cheese tin without its top and bottom. Place over it the plate which must never touch the water. (You can use a steamer)

While the crab is being steamed, minced the meat. Chop into pieces of 1 cm the Chinese garlic, in match sticks the bamboo shoots, the "Tong Ku" and the mushrooms. After 20 minutes, remove the crab meat.

Pour into a pan, 2 measures of oil on a fierce heat, add 1 pinch of salt and the crab, stir 60 seconds. Add in the meat and stir for 30 seconds. Remove and place in a large plate. Add some more oil and fry the mushrooms and the "Tong Ku".

In a large bowl, put the crab meat, the Chinese garlic, the bamboo shoots, 1 spoonful of salt, 1 spoonful of ajinomoto, 6 spoonfuls of starch. Mix well to make the farce meat.

The Dough:

For ½ kg of sieved flour, 125 gms of dripping, ½ teaspoonful of table salt and ¾ cup of water. Knead and divide into five parts. Take one part and shape in a long piece of 25 cm. Fold in the "stick" to obtain a rectangle of pastry of 45 × 12 cm.

Put the meat in the middle. Make a roll of about 4 cm diameter. Stick with some water the two ends. Repeat the operation for the four other parts.

Cooking:

Pour out the oil into a pan and slide in a roll. Fry, turning the roll from time to time until golden. Repeat for the others.

Serve hot with hot pepper garlic sauce.

Fried Veal with Jamaica Pepper and Cucumber

Ingredients:

½ kg of veal

1 small cucumber

3 — 4 Jamaica peppers

Salt, pepper and ajinomoto

1 tablespoonful of starch (corn flour)

1 tablespoonful of siaw sauce

Some white wine

2 chopped garlic pods, and some ginger cut into pieces.

Oil

Preparation:

Remove from the meat the nerves and the fat. Cut into large slices and with the Chinese knife handle hammer them. Cut into small pieces, taking care to cut slant-wise. Place the meat in a bowl. Add some starch, pepper, ajinomoto and the siaw sauce, mix and leave for 15 — 20 minutes. Cut the peppers into 8 long pieces. Take out the seeds.

Peel the cucumber and cut into sticks of 1½ inches. Dissolve the rest of the starch in 2 spoonfuls of white wine.

Cooking:

Warm 2 measures of oil in Chinese wok. Fry for 10 seconds the garlic and ginger. Then add the peppers. Fry for 20 seconds. Remove from oil and keep warm. Put in the cucumber and fry for 30 seconds. Stirring continuously. Remove.

Stir in the meat. Then add the dissolved starch powder. Cook for some 3 minutes on fierce heat, stirring continuously. Then add the peppers and the cucumber. Stir for another 20 seconds and remove from heat.

Serve as an appertizer or with rice and a tomato chutney.

Squash and Braised Meat

Ingredients:

4 squash (patisson)

250 gms of tender meat (beef or pork)

1 teaspoonful of "dowsee"

Salt, pepper, ajinomoto, ginger, garlic and starch

Oil

Preparation:

Cut into pieces the meat and the squash. Mix with the chopped garlic and ginger. Blend some siaw sauce, the starch and ajinomoto.

Cooking:

Warm 2 measures of oil in a Chinese wok, brown a piece of ginger. Put into the squash. Brown for 1 minute, add ¼ cup of water. Cover and cook on moderate heat for 12 minutes. Pour the prepared mixture on the beef and mix well. Then stir in the meat on the squash without crushing the squash. Cover and simmer for another 7 minutes. Mix well before serving.

Fried Beef Liver with Cauliflower

Ingredients:

½ kg of beef liver

1 white cauliflower

4 garlic pods

1 piece of chopped ginger

1 tablespoonful of starch (corn flour)

1 tablespoonful of siaw sauce

1 pinch of salt, pepper and ajinomoto

2 chopped Bombay onions

Oil

Preparation:

Cut the liver into small slices, taking care to remove beforehand the film covering the liver and slicing the meat slant-wise. Place the pieces into plate, add pepper, siaw sauce, the starch and the ajinomoto. Break the cauliflower into small flowers.

Cooking:

Pour some oil into a wok, brown the garlic and the ginger. Stir in the liver preferably with a Chinese spatula. Cook for 5 — 7 minutes. Stirring from time to time. Then add the cauliflower and stir for another 2 minutes. Then add the Bombay onions and cook for 2 minutes and remove from heat.

Serve with rice and a tomato chutney.

Bean Sprouts

Used in numerous meals and are of great nutritive value. Serve very well in omelettes, stews, fried noodles, and others.

To Obtain Soya Beans:

In a wooden box, place a piece of cloth, of a bigger size than the bottom of the box. The box must be scrupulously clean. Soak into water for a night, 125 gms of soya beans. Place the jute piece of cloth at the bottom.

Soak it with water and place on it the soya beans. Cover well with the four sides of the piece of cloth, the soya beans. Avoid by all means the light to penetrate the beans; for then, the shoots will be tough green and will grow leaves and will not be edible.

Put the box into a damp place, press the jute with some stones, water 3 times daily (morning, noon, night). Leave for 5 days but do not uncover. After that, the sprouts should be ready.

Cooked Pork with Bean Sprouts

Ingredients:

½ kg of soya bean sprouts

125 gms of green Chinese peas "Sep-tev"

*125 gms of "Wun-Yee" or "Cloud ears"
(mushrooms)*

250 gms lean pork

1 Bombay onion

1 tablespoonful of starch (Corn flour)

1 spoonful of honey

1 spoonful of sugar

Salt, pepper and ajinomoto

2 garlic pods

2 spoonfuls of white wine

Oil

Preparation:

Cut the pork into small pieces along the grain, mix with some starch, honey and 1 spoonful of siaw sauce, ajinomoto, pepper and some oil. Let it marinade for ½ hour.

Mix the starch, 2 spoonfuls of water, 1 spoonful of sugar and some siaw sauce.

Wash and soak the "Wun-Yee", wash the soya beans, removing the protective films and the roots.

Cooking:

Warm some oil in a Chinese wok. Brown the onion, cut into 4, and then the "Sep-tev", the "Wung-Yee" stir continuously on a fierce heat. Cover with a wooden lid and cook on a moderate heat for 2 minutes.

Remove from heat and keep warm. Add some more oil, if necessary, brown the chopped garlic, add the pork and stir fry for another minute. Cover and cook for 3 minutes. Then add the vegetables and mix. Make a well in the middle and stir in the starch. As soon as the sauce becomes thick enough, mix with a Chinese spatula. Avoid crushing the vegetables, cover and add 2 spoonfuls of white wine. Simmer for 2 — 3 minutes.

Serve hot with rice.

Pork, Palm Tree Heart or Bamboo Shoots

The palm tree heart is a nice vegetable that is usually served in a salad or in a hot spicy sauce called "Hot Pickle". It can be replaced easily by bamboo shoots which can be found fresh in some local markets.

Ingredients:

1 kg of young pork

½ palm heart or bamboo or again
*   1 tin of bamboo shoots*

125 gms of washed soya bean sprouts

Salt, pepper, ajinomoto, starch
*   (corn flour), red wine and siaw sauce*

1 chopped Bombay onion

½ cup of milk

3 garlic pods or 1 piece of ginger

Oil

Preparation:

On a Chinese wooden chopping slab, cut into small pieces the meat, put them into a bowl, add 2 spoonfuls of starch, 1 spoonful of pepper, some ajinomoto, mix well and leave for 1 hour at least.

Cut the palm heart into small pieces put the pieces in a pan of water with some milk. Drain before cooking.

Cooking:

Pour out 2 measures of oil in a Chinese wok. Brown some pepper, add in the pieces of palm heart. Stir continuously until golden. Remove from heat and keep warm.

Brown the sprouts taking care to keep the shoots well apart with the help of a fork. As soon as they are cooked, remove from heat and keep warm in a bowl. If necessary, add some more oil in the wok, warm until very hot. Brown the garlic and the ginger for 10 seconds. Add the pork and fry, keeping the pieces on the sides of the wok. Stir from time to time, add some water, cover with a wooden lid, fry for 10 minutes, stirring occasionally. Then add in the soya beans, and the pieces of palm heart. Mix well.

In the meantime, prepare the sauce with 1 spoonful of siaw sauce, 1 spoonful of starch and 2 spoonfuls of red wine. Make a well in the middle of the ingredients in the pan. Pour in the sauce and let it get thick. Mix vigorously, add the Bombay onion and cook for 3 — 4 minutes.

You can replace the pork by chicken and you can add some Chinese mushrooms fried separately.

Braised Pork and Egg-Plants Cooked in Chinese Fashion

Ingredients:

250 gms of long and thin egg-plants
250 gms of fat pork
1 spoonful of "Sang See Yeung" sauce
1 teaspoonful of siaw sauce
Sugar, salt, pepper and ajinomoto
1 tablespoonful of starch
1 piece of finely chopped ginger
3 garlic pods
Oil

Preparation:

Halve the egg-plants and cut again into 4 so as to have 8 pieces from 1 egg-plant. Do not peel. Chop the garlic and the ginger. Cut the pork into pieces. Mix with the "Sang See Yeung" sauce, salt, siaw, pepper, ajinomoto and starch. Marinade for ½ hour.

Cooking:

Warm 2 measures of oil in a Chinese Wok. Fry the ginger and garlic. Stir in the egg-plants. Brown while stirring continuously for 4 minutes. Remove from oil and keep warm. If necessary, pour in some more oil. Fry the pork for 2 minutes, add ½ cup of boiling water, cover and simmer for 5 minutes. Uncover and then add the egg-plants and cook for another 5 minutes.

Serve hot with rice.

Beef and Pork with Sep-Tev

Ingredients:

250 gms of veal
250 gms of tender pork meat
250 gms of "Sep-Tev" small garden Chinese peas with hull (mange-tout)
Salt, pepper and ajinomoto
1 tablespoonful of siaw sauce
1 tablespoonful of starch, diluted in red wine
2 Bombay onions
1 piece of finely sliced ginger
4 garlic pods finely chopped
Oil

Preparation:

Remove the nerves from the beef meat and cut into small pieces along the grain. Add some starch, the siaw sauce and the ajinomoto. Mix well and leave for 20 minutes. Wash the "Sep-Tev" keeping them whole. Chop the Bombay onions.

Cooking:

Warm 2 measures of oil in Chinese Wok, brown the garlic and ginger. Put in the meat and fry while stirring for 4 — 5 minutes. In the middle of the cooking, add the "Sep-Tev". Cook for 2 minutes. Some minutes before removing from heat, add the onions. The "Sep-Tev" must stay green but cooked.

Serve with rice.

Beef/Pork/Chicken Meat and Chinese Green (Chop-Soy)

In the Chinese sections of our local markets, you can easily find the different varieties of Chinese greens. The secrets of a well — Cooked green is to avoid over-cooking and for that, you need a fierce heat.

Ingredients:

250 gms of beef or pork or chicken
3 bunches of Chinese greens
1 tablespoonful of starch
Salt, pepper and ajinomoto
3 garlic pods, crushed
1 piece of ginger, crushed
Oil

Preparation:

Cut the meat into small pieces, mix with 1 spoonful of starch, pepper and ajinomoto. Leave for 1 hour. Cut your greens into pieces of 2 — 3 inches and wash.

Cooking:

Pour out 2 measures of oil in a Chinese wok. Brown the chopped garlic and ginger. Then add the meat and cook. When the meat is cooked, add the greens and mix well. At the same time, add the sauce made of 1 spoonful of starch, 1 spoonful of siaw and some water. Mix vigorously and remove as soon as the greens are cooked.

Serve with hot rice and hot pepper tomato chutney.

The Upturned Rice Bowl

This is a rice meal, pleasant to sight and easy to prepare.

Ingredients:

5 measures of rice

½ kg of boned chicken

250 gms of lean pork

125 gms of Chinese sausages

100 gms of Chinese mushrooms

3 tablespoonfuls of starch

½ cup of red wine

1 bunch of coriander

Salt, pepper, ajinomoto, chopped garlic and ginger,

Cinnamon

Oil

Preparation:

Cook the rice in a rice-cooker in 9 measures of water, adding 1 stick of cinnamon. Cut into very small pieces the chicken and the pork. Mix in ½ of starch, the ajinomoto, the pepper and leave for ½ hour.

Cut the sausages into slanted slices. Soak the mushrooms and wash. Make a sauce with the wine, the rest of the starch and some pepper.

Cooking:

Pour the measures of oil in a Chinese wok. Brown the mushrooms for 2 minutes. Remove and keep warm. Fry the sausages in hot oil for 30 seconds, remove and keep warm. If necessary, add some oil and put the garlic, brown for 10 seconds. Add the pork and chicken meat. Cover with a wooden lid and cook for 5 minutes. Uncover, add some hot water, stir and cook for another 3 minutes.

Uncover and make a well in the middle of the meat, pour in the wine sauce. Mix. Then add the mushrooms and the sausages. Mix. The sauce must not be too thick or too watery.

Choose a large Chinese bowl (15 cm diameter). Cover the bottom with chopped coriander leaves, then put in the meat, the sausage, then the rice piled up to the brim. Place a plate over with your left hand and the bowl in the right.

Reverse the bowl on the plate and remove bowl in front of your guest.

Serve with a tomato chutney.

Yam Cake (Voo Yan)

Ingredients:

1 kg of yam (arouille)
125 gms of ginger
1 tablespoonful of corn flour
1 tablespoonful of siaw
1 teaspoonful of ajinomoto
2 pinches of salt
Oil for deep frying

Preparation & Cooking:

Grate the yam (after peeling). Peel the ginger and grate it.

Press the grated yam between both hands to remove the juice. Mix in all the other ingredients. Make the mixture in small balls and deep fry.

Serve with a hot chillies sauce.

INDIAN CUISINE

Typical "Haldi" Menu.

Briani

The Briani is a typical Muslim meal, appreciated by everyone in this country, the meat can be beef, deer, chicken or goat or else meaty fish (like tuna).

Ingredients (for 12):

2 kg of long grain rice

2 kg of meat

1 kg of black lentils

125 gms of garlic

250 gms of ginger

Some oriental saffron (Jaffrane)

2 kg of onions

4 bunches of coriander leaves

4 bunches of garden mint

7 pieces of nutmeg

125 gms of cumin seeds

17 grains of cardamom

Small quantity of oriental colouring (yellow)

1 bottle of milk curd or sour milk

12 eggs

40 cl of frying oil

2 lemons

50 cl of water

2 tablespoonfuls of salt

125 gms of ghee

Cooking Ustensils:

2 pans of 30 cm diameter.

Preparation:

To cook this meal is a very elaborate one but it brings so much satisfaction that it is worthwhile trying. It is advisable to prepare in advance as much as possible the ingredients, and to start very early in the morning (6.00 am).

Curd the milk by boiling it at least 12 hours beforehand with lemons. As soon as the milk is curdled, put it in the fridge.

Clean carefully the rice and the lentils separately.

Pod the onions and the garlic.

Cut the meat into dices of 4/5 cm. If you use chicken, make use rather of 2 unleaved chickens. In case of fish, remove carefully all the bones.

Grind the garlic.

Grind the ginger and press it in a clean cloth to obtain the juice.

Dilute the colorant in 2 tablespoonfuls of hot water.

Chop finely the garden mint and the coriander. Grill the aniseeds; grind it with 5 pieces of nutmeg and the 13 grains of cumin seeds.

Fry the 2 kgs of sliced onions in ghee.

The next operation is called the "Battle" because the hand beats the paste by regular beats in a pan. Mix the 12 following ingredients, and beat them.

The ground garlic, the ginger juice, the saffron threads, the mint and coriander leaves, 1 kg of fried onions. The beef pieces, whole peppers, the curdled milk, 4 tablespoonfuls of ghee. The frying oil and 1 tablespoonful of salt.

Allow those 12 ingredients to macertate. All depending on the tenderness of the meat (chicken is to stay 1 hour or 2; malagasy beef for 4 — 5 hours, fish ½ hour; for the idea is to cook the meat "outside the fire."

Fill ¾ with fresh water one of the dectis, throw in the rest of the nutmeg and the cumin seeds, and the salt. Bring to the boil, throw in the rice, bring to the boil once more, count up to 5, remove and strain.

Infuse the oriental saffron in ½ cup of boiling water and strain.

Potatoes: Peel the potatoes and put them in the infusion to give them colour and perfume. Take them away from the water and fry them into the ghee.

Lentils: Bring to the boil the pulses and half allow to cook.

Eggs: Boil the eggs, shell them, fry in the remaining ghee.

Cooking:

Cover the bottom of the pan with a layer of rice, this rice will not serve as it will prevent the briani from burning.

Cover it then, with a layer of the mixture that you will have allowed to macerate in such a way that the rice is evenly spread on the first layer.

Evenly spread the potatoes and the eggs.

Cover with 15 mm of rice.

Sprinkle on this rice some of the oriental saffron and also some fried onions, black pulses and some drops of ghee.

Spray a layer of meat and repeat until the exhaustion of all your ingredients.

Pour in 2 small bottles of water. Seal the pan with some flour paste along the lid, cook on a small fire for 2 hours.

To serve — Remove the last layer of rice and serve with the meat, vegetables and eggs.

Serve with an assortment of chutneys — made of cucumber and grated carrots.

Vendillion Curry

This is a typical spicy Madras curry; people who suffer from stomach problems should refrain from eating this meal. Like all the other curries, it should be cooked in the wok after the preparation of all the necessary ingredients:

Ingredients (for 6):

½ kg of bomeli fish (Bombay duck)

100 gms garlic

4 — 5 bay leaves, 3 of fennel, some (metti)

6 big red tomatoes

4 tamarind balls

Juice from 2 lemons

Gram massala ground and water used for the grinding

250 gms of onions cut into 4

5 — 6 small egg-plants (the smelting green cover at the top should be removed but not the sticks)

1 tablespoonful of ajinomoto

6 chillies cut lengthwise

1 bunch of coriander leaves

Oil

Preparation & Cooking:

Put in a Chinese wok on a medium fire, add three measures of oil. When the oil is hot, fry the bomeli fish (that you will have cleaned carefully beforehand). Remove fish when fried, keep warm in a bowl. In the same oil, fry the small egg-plants whole, taking care not to crush them; when well fried remove from oil and keep warm.

Add some more oil, and warm, brown the (metti) then the whole garlic pods, then add the onions, the bay leaves, fennel, then the gram massala whisk vigorously. Add by tablespoonful, the water and brown. You can also add the warm water in which the tamarind will have diluted. When well-cooked, that is when the massala and oil are separated or when the smell is that of cooked massala, stir in the tomatoes and allow them to simmer in the sauce, until they are diluted in the sauce, add then the fried bomeli fish and egg-plants cook for 4 — 5 minutes. Put them in a pyrex plate, add the coriander, stir in well, cover and uncover only when ready to serve.

The Bomeli fish can be replaced by boiled eggs, and small shrimps, which must be fried like the bomeli fish.

Kaliah

This is a very spicy meal prepared by the Muslims. The meat used is mutton or deer or goat or beef.

Ingredients:

½ kg tender meat

2 tablespoonfuls of ground ginger and garlic

1 teaspoonful of table salt

1 teaspoonful of ground nutmeg

1 tablespoonful of ajinomoto

1 pinch of cardamom

1 small tablespoonful of aniseeds

40 cl of curdled milk

4 — 5 onions chopped finely

Some jaffrane

1 tablespoonful of ghee or table oil

4 boiled eggs (scalded)

6 small boiled potatoes

Preparation:

Clean the meat, remove all the nerves and dice. Mix the meat in a bowl with the ginger, pepper, nutmeg, cloves, salt, ajinomoto, cardamom, aniseeds, onions, ghee and the curdled milk.

Mix well and marinade for 3 — 4 hours. Fry in the ghee the eggs, and the whole potatoes.

Cooking:

On a very mild heat, cook the meat for 2 hours stirring from time to time. The cooking is better on a charcoal fire and place on the lid of the saucepan some burning charcoal. Half hour before serving, add the eggs and the potatoes well roasted in the ghee. Dilute the jaffrane in some hot water and add the sauce some minutes before serving. Uncover before serving.

Dhansack Chicken

This is a parsi meal (North India). The word means chicken dholl.

Ingredients (for 5):

5 measures of basmati rice
1 kg of young chicken
250 gms of minced meat (Beef)
1 pinch of cinnamon
100 gms of sugar
125 gms of dholl
3 — 4 Bombay onions
1 measure of sultana
5 — 6 nutmegs
3 — 4 small tender egg-plants
250 gms of pumpkin
125 gms of ground massala
1 small tin of ghee
1 egg
2 small onions
Oil

Preparation & Cooking:

Cook the rice in the rice cooker (for 5 measures of rice, 8 measures of water). Melt 3 tablespoonfuls of ghee in a pan, add in small quantities 100 gms of white sugar and 1 tablespoonful of ground cinnamon until a creamy sauce is obtained. Mix this sauce to the rice, using a fork to prevent the crushing of rice. Put back the pan, add some ghee, fry the Bombay onions until they are of a nice colour, mix in the oil, the sultanas and the nutmeg. Remove the onions, nutmegs and sultanas will decorate the rice, or else mix the sultanas in the rice.

Cooking of the Dholl:

Put the dholl in cold water, some salt, the egg-plants cut into half and the diced pumpkin in a pressure cooker for 15 minutes. When cooked, mince the dholl and the vegetables to obtain a paste that you will brown in some oil and onion.

Cooking of the Chicken:

Cut into pieces the chicken, season with the pepper and the salt. Boil these pieces for 3 — 4 minutes in hot water. In a Chinese wok, melt 2 tablespoonfuls of ghee, put 100 gms of massala in the melted ghee and brown. When the massala and the grease separate promptly, add in the chicken and some of the water in which the chicken has been boiled. Cook on small heat for 10 minutes.

The Meat Balls:

Chop finely the onions, mix in the minced meat, add the rest of the massala and an egg, a pinch of flour. Macerate in the massala for 1 hour, knead the meat into small balls that you will deep fry.

You must time everything so that the meat balls, chicken meat, dholl and rice are ready at almost the same time.

You can proceed in this way:

— Prepare the meat for the meat balls.

— Cook the rice in the cooker and the dholl in the pressure cooker.

— Boil the chicken and prepare the massala.

— Prepare the sauce with the sugar, the ghee and the nutmeg, and mix in the rice as soon as the latter is cooked, keep in the rice cooker. Open when ready to serve.

— In the Chinese wok, fry the onions, the sultanas, and the nuts. Serve in a long plate and decorate with onions.

— Fry the meat balls and place them around the chicken in another dish. Serve the dholl in saucers.

Dhall Pita

This is a typical Indian meal which can be compared with some imagination to the Italian ravioli.

Ingredients (for 6):

½ kg of dholl
½ kg of flour
Some garlic pods
4 — 5 pieces of ground saffron
Some ginger
4 big onions
3 — 4 red chillies
Salt and ajinomoto
2 tablespoonfuls of ghee

Preparation & Cooking:

Grind together garlic, ginger and chillies. Melt the ghee in a pressure cooker. Brown the ground spices for 45 seconds. Brown the ground saffron until the ghee and the saffron separate.

Add the well-washed dholl, turn continuously, add some hot water or stock to cover your dholl. Close the pressure cooker and allow to whistle. At the first whistle, lower the fire and cook for another 5 minutes. Remove cooker from heat and uncover. Beforehand you will have prepared a paste with some flour, some salt, 1 tablespoonful of oil and fresh water. The paste must be firm. Roll into balls that you will later flatten into small disks called small faratas. Put into the dholl the faratas and cook for 20 minutes. Brown the onions in some ghee and add them to your dhall pita. Add ajinomoto, stir for some minutes and serve. Serve with a coconut chutney.

You can replace the "small farata" by plain ravioli.

Mango Kutcha

The word kutcha is derived from the Indian word kuntch which means to crush.

It is a kind of vegetable curry that ought to be eaten after the cooking but can be kept in the fridge for a week or more. It can be served hot as a curry.

Ingredients:

1 dozen of green mangoes

6 big peppers

125 gms of saffron (green)

6 garlic pods

2 pieces of ginger

½ cup of vinegar

Salt, pepper and ajinomoto

6 halved small onions

40 cl of mustard oil (or ordinary oil and 1 teaspoonful of ground mustard)

Preparation:

Peel the mangoes. Pound or grate the mangoes. Grind the saffron.

Cooking:

Warm the oil in a Chinese wok; brown the garlic and the ginger for 20 seconds, then add the ground saffron diluted in ½ cup of white vinegar, brown for another 30 seconds. Add the chillies, brown for 20 seconds. Stirring continuously. Add the mango paste and cook for only 1 minute. Add then a tablespoonful of ground mustard, if you have used ordinary oil, salt and ajinomoto, and serve.

Typical Ingredients
for Curries and Chutneys.

Toukra or Spicy Scotch Eggs

This is an exotic Muslim meal, with great nutritive values and very spicy.

Ingredients (for 6):

½ kg of minced meat
6 boiled eggs
2 eggs uncooked
6 garlic pods
4 small peppers
250 gms of onions
1 bunch of coriander
1 tablespoonful of Bezan flour
2 cardamoms
1 cup of curdled milk
6 big green peppers
3 tomatoes
1 tablespoonful of ground massala
1 tablespoonful of ground saffron
1 tablespoonful of ground coriander seeds
1 tablespoonful of ground red pepper
1 tablespoonful of aniseeds
1 tablespoonful of tomato paste
250 gms of ghee

Preparation & Cooking:

Ground in a mortar, some ginger, 3 clovers and 2 onions; mix in the meat that you will cook with a cup of water and ½ tablespoonful of saffron and some salt. Simmer until the meat is tender, add the besan or 1 tablespoonful of maizena. Stir continuously for 5 minutes until there is no water left. Remove from heat, mix in the uncooked egg and the massala powder. Make the toukra by covering a boiled egg with a layer of minced meat. Melt 250 gms of ghee in a wok. Put the koftas in a whisked egg. Fry in very hot ghee until they are brown. Remove the toukra and keep warm. In the remaining ghee, fry the rest of the onions, add the green peppers, the ground coriander, aniseeds, the rest of the saffron, 3 garlic pods, the ground pepper, fry until red; add the tomato paste, brown then add the minced tomatoes and some hot water; simmer for 5 minutes. Stir in the whisked curdled milk, bring to a boil and cook for 15 minutes on a mild heat. Add the chopped coriander. Serve with rice and fried salted fish.

Tandoori Chicken

The tandoori chicken is cooked traditionally in a tandour, a sort of clay oven, but an electrical or gas oven can also be used.

Ingredients:

1 chicken of 1 kg in quarter
40 cl of curdled milk
50 gms of massala (special for tandouri)
1 pinch of oriental colour (red)
Salt and ajinomoto

Preparation:

Soak the chicken for 12 hours in curdled milk added with salt.

Remove the chicken, strain and rub with massala paste to which colour has been added. Let macerate for at least 1 hour.

Cooking:

Warm the oven, hang the quarters of chicken by a small hook at the top of the oven. Close the door. Bring down the temperature to moderate heat and allow to cook for 30 minutes. Remove and serve with a green salad with faratas.

Vindaloo Chicken

The next recipe is the hottest curry I know; it is therefore not advisable for those who suffer from stomach aches. Serve the vindaloo chicken with rice and red bordeaux wine.

Ingredients:

1 kg of tender chicken (cut into pieces)

3 cups of white vinegar

5 tablespoonfuls of ground coriander seeds

2 tablespoonfuls of ground red pepper

2 tablespoonfuls of aniseeds

1½ tablespoonfuls of mustard seeds

1 tablespoonful of ground saffron

1 tablespoonful of black pepper

12 garlic pods

1 piece of cinnamon

1 piece of ginger

Salt and oil

Preparation:

Grind the spices, salt, pepper, garlic, ginger, nutmeg and mustard. Dilute the paste in vinegar. Mix the ground spices to obtain an homogenous paste. Add some vinegar if the paste is too hard.

Cooking:

Warm 40 cl of oil in a Chinese wok, remove the wok from the fire, allow to cool. Put in all the paste, stir and put the wok back on the fire — cook for another 12 minutes until the paste takes a red colour. Then fry in the chicken pieces for 10 minutes until all the vinegar and oil is absorbed. Then add 2 cups of stock, and cook on moderate heat for another 10 minutes.

Halim

A typical Muslim meal; a consistent meal and that does not cost much.

Ingredients:

6 goat legs cleaned

½ kg of goat meat

2 measures of dholl

1 measure of broken wheat

2 bunches of coriander leaves

Spices:

2 tablespoonfuls of coriander seeds

1 tablespoonful of elaiti (Cardamom)

1 tablespoonful of aniseeds

1 piece of ginger

10 garlic pods

1 tablespoonful of ground pepper

6 large red peppers

3 small onions, some cloves
  and cinnamon.

Oil

Preparation:

Grind the spices mentioned and keep the water used for the grinding. Clean the goat's legs and dice the meat. Chop finely the coriander.

Cooking:

Put the legs and meat in a pressure cooker, add some salt and ajinomoto, some cloves and piece of cinnamon. Cover everything with cold water, cook under pressure for 2 hours, open the cooker, and remove the bones.

In another cooker, warm 2 measures of oil. Put the ground spices and brown. Stirring continuously, add in small quantities the water. When the massala gets separated from the oil, put the dholl, brown and add some hot water, stir and brown for 3 — 4 minutes. Transfer the contents to a pressure cooker, bring to boil, add boiling water to fill the cooker on the ¾. Close and cook under pressure for 20 minutes. Open and add the broken wheat — cook for another 5 minutes, put in the coriander. Serve as a soup with lemon, pepper and tomato sauce.

Serve with bread or rice.

Moulougtany

The moulougtany, spiced soup comes from Madras. Moulouga — spices, tanni — sauce.

Ingredients:

1 chicken of 1 kg
6 fresh water shrimps or a small lobster
1 measure of dholl
½ kg of dasheen leaves
4 small egg-plants
1 tablespoonful of aniseeds
1 tablespoonful of mustard seeds
1 tablespoonful of ground pepper
2 garlic pods
6 pieces of ginger
4 small onions
6 bay leaves
1 bunch of coriander leaves
3 tamarind balls.
2 pieces of dried saffron

Preparation:

Cut the chicken into pieces, clean the shrimps or lobster. Soak the dholl, peel the dasheen and cut into pieces; cut the egg-plants into pieces, mince the coriander and soak the tamarind balls. Grind all the spices in order to make a paste.

Cooking:

Take a large pressure cooker, warm a measure of oil, brown the massala paste, add the water by tablespoonful until the oil and the massala get separated. Then add the dholl, the dasheen leaves and the egg-plants. Cook for another 5 minutes while stirring and add some hot water if necessary. Stir in the shrimps/lobster and the chicken. Brown in the sauce for another 5 minutes, stirring for some minutes. Add some hot water, to fill the cooker. Close and cook under pressure for 1 hour.

Uncover, add salt if necessary and the chopped coriander leaves.

Serve in soup bowls.

Pilau

Easy to cook.

Ingredients:

5 measures of rice
½ kg of pork diced
5 pieces of chicken (legs or breast)
10 sausages
Oil

Spices:

4 pieces of dried saffron
1 garlic pod
1 piece of ginger
4 large red pepper
4 small onions
3 fennels (4 epices)

Preparation & Cooking:

Warm 1 measure of oil in the pressure cooker, brown the spice paste until the oil and spices get separated, put in the pork, cook for some 3 minutes. Then add the chicken and cook for some more minutes, add some water, close the cooker and cook for 10 minutes. Transfer to the rice cooker, add 5 measures of rice and 8 measures of water in which the saffron will have been diluted. Mix well. Start the rice cooker and allow to cook. As soon as the signal ready is on, add the sausages, already steamed.

Mix well and serve.

Kat-Lesse

Another Muslim meal — served as a hors d'oeuvre.

Ingredients (for 15 Kat-Lesse):

½ kg of meat (beef, goat or mutton)
5 large onions
10 spring onions with leaves
Some coriander leaves and mint leaves
5 eggs
Salt and ajinomoto
Breadcrumbs
Cumin
Oil

Preparation:

Mince the meat. Chop the onions finely with coriander leaves.

In a large bowl, add to the meat, onions, the coriander and mint leaves, the cumin, the salt, 1 tablespoonful of ajinomoto, 2 eggs, knead until a smooth paste is obtained.

Cooking:

Pour out some oil in a wok. On the other hand, put some breadcrumbs in a large plate, take some meat in your hand, make out small round, flat cakes, sprinkle with breadcrumbs — you should obtain 12 — 17 kat-lesse

In a large bowl, break the 3 remaining eggs, whisk, when oil is very hot, pass rapidly the kat-lesse into the eggs, and then deep fry.

Serve with chips.

Dholl Croquettes or Chilli Bites

Ingredients:

½ kg of dholl (avoid the pigeon peas for
    they tend to be bitter)

10 large peppers

3 tablespoonfuls of flour

1 tablespoonful of ajinomoto

12 large leaves of drum sticks

1 small bunch of spring onions

10 large onions chopped finely

A pinch of bicarbonate

Oil

Preparation:

Soak the dholl to be used overnight. Wash to remove the starch. Put in a sieve and wash in clean water.

Grind the dholl on the grinding slab or electric mixer.

Mix in a large bowl, the ground dholl, the onions, the minced leaves, the flour, the starch, the ajinomoto, the spring onions, 1 tablespoonful of unrefined salt. Make a homogenous paste.

Cooking:

Warm some oil in a wok. Deep fry the croquettes having made it in the form of a small doughnut.

Vegetable Preserved

Economical and handy for every Mauritian housewife. When the vegetables are cheap, they are prepared in large quantities, well-cooked and well preserved in sterilized pots. They can remain for weeks and months. The appropriate vegetables are: cauliflower, cabbage, green beans, carrot.

Ingredients:

1 nice cauliflower

½ kg of carrots

1 cabbage

½ kg of green beans

250 gms of green saffron

8 garlic pods

125 gms of ginger

Salt

10 large green chillies

40 cl of mustard oil

1 tablespoonful of ajinomoto

½ cup of vinegar

Preparation:

Clean the carrots, and cut them into sticks. Halve the beans. Cut the cabbage leaves. Peel the onions. Grind the green saffron, the ginger and garlic. Mix these spices in the vinegar and ajinomoto.

As for the vegetables, they should be put in the sun for 2 days, they must not be too dry.

Cooking:

Warm the mustard oil in a Chinese wok; add the diluted saffron, brown for some minutes. Then add the large green peppers and the onions. Brown for 20 seconds; add the vegetables. Mix well, if necessary, add some hot oil. Mix and cook for 3 minutes. Stir from time to time.

Glossary

Ajinomoto (sodium monoglutamate):

Powder or crystals used more especially in Chinese cuisine to highlight taste of some dishes.

Choy Sam (or ham choy):

Preserved Chinese cabbage.

Dow See:

Special flavouring Chinese sauce.

Haldi Menu:

Dinner served after the Hindu tradition on the night preceding a marriage celebration.

Heung New Fun:

5 spices special Chinese powder.

A pinch:

Quantity taken by the first three fingers of the hand.

Rice cooker measure:

Small plastic container obtained when you buy a rice cooker. This measure holds the exact quantity of rice needed to feed a normal adult at one meal.

Sang See Jeung:

Special Chinese spice.

Siaw sauce (or soya sauce):

Sauce made of soya beans used in numerous dishes to give colour as well as taste.

Starch (or corn flour):

Special flour used for thickening sauces.

Tong Ku:

Dried Chinese mushrooms which must be soaked in water and softened before use.

Twist of Oil (or measure of oil):

Hold a bottle of oil and with a sudden twist of the wrist describe as a "circle" of oil in the wok.

Wung Yee (cloud ears):

Same as Tong Ku but of different shape.

List of Vegetables

English	Patois Creole	French	Indian	Scientific
Ash gourd	Patol	Patol		Trichosanthes anguina
Beetroot	Betterave	Betterave	Chukander	Beta vulgaris
Bitter gourd	Margoses	Margoses	Karela	Momordica charanti
Bread fruit	Fruit à pain (madegone)	Fruit à pain	Badhal	Aertocarpus incisa
Cabbage	Chou	Chou	Gobi	Brassico claecera var capitata
Cauliflower	Choufleur	Chou fleur	Phool erbi	Brassica oleracea
Carrots	Carotte	Carotte	Gajar	Dacus carota
Cassava	Manioc	Manioc		Manihot utilissima
Chinese cabbage	Brede petsai	Chou de chine	Petsai	Brasicea chiniencis
Cucumber	Concombre	Concombre	Kakri	Cucumis satavis
Cho cho (Choyote)	Chou chou	Chou chou		Sechium edule
Dholl	Dholl	Dholl	Ar how	Pisum sativum
Drum stick	Mouroum (baton)	Mourouc	Surjani ki sem	Moringa pterygosperma robusta
Gourd	Calebas	Calebasse	Kaddu	Lagenaria vulgaris
Indian mustard	Brede de chine	Brede moutarde	Aba	Baassica juncea
Jack fruit	Jac	Jac	Kathal	Artocarpus integrifolia
Ladies fingers	Lalo	Lalo	Bindhi	Hibiscus esculenta
Love apple/tomato	Pommes d'amour	Tomates	Tamatare	Lycopersicum esculentum
Mushrooms	Champignon	Champignon		
Passiflora	Grenadine (carri)	Barbadine	Rata cumul	Passiflora quadrangularis
Pigeons peas	Embrevade (bravat)	Embrevade	Burbut	Cajanus indica
Potatoes	Pomme de terre	Pomme de terre	Alu	Solanum tuberosum
Red beans	Haricots rouge	Haricots rouge	Rajma	Phaseolus vulgaris
Red pumpkin	Giraumon	Giraumon	Konra	Cucurbita pepo
Sponge gourd	Pipengaille	Pipengaille	Taroi	Luffa acutangula
Spinach	Epinard	Epinard	Palak	Spinacia oleracea
Taro/dasheen leaves	Brede songe	Brède songe	Kachu bhaji	Colocasia antiguoram
Turnip	Navet	Navet	Shalgam	Brassica rapa
Turnip cabbage	Chou navet	Chou navet	Shalgam	Brassica sp
Water cress	Brede cresson	Cresson	Kannutu pala	Nasturtium officinale

List of Spices, Seasonings Herbs, etc

English	Patois Creole	French	Indian	Scientific
Capsicum	Pima (gros)	Gros piment	Mirch	Capsicum spp
Caraway	Gros l'anis	Anis	Saün	Carum carvi
Cardamom	Laiti	Cardamome	Elaichi	Elletteria cardamonum
Chillies	P'tit piment	Piment	Simla mirch	Capsicum minimum
Cinnamon	Kanel	Cannelle	Delchini	Cinnomonium zeylanicum
Coriander	Cotomili	Coriandre	Dhania	Coriandrum sativum
Cumin seed	P'tit l'anis	Cumin	Jeera	Cuminum cyminum
Curry leaves	Carri poulet	Feuilles à carri	Khadi patta	Murraya koenigii
Coconut	Coco	Coco	Neriel	Cocos nucifera
Curd milk	Dilait caillé	Lait caillé	Dahi	
Dill	Soa	Soa	Shuva rhaji	Peucedanum graveolens
Garlic	L'ail	Ail	Lansen	Allium sativum
Ginger	Zinzam	Gingembre	Adrak	Zingiber officinale
Fenugreek	Meti	Trigonelle	Methi	Trigonella foenum-graecum
Jaffrane	Jaffranne	Safran orientale	Kesar	Crocus sativus
Mustard	La moutarde	Moutarde	Rai (sarso)	Brassica alba
Nutmeg	Muscad	Muscade	Jaifal	Myristica fragrans
Onions	Zoignons	Oignons	Piaj	Allium cepa
Parsley	Persi	Persi	Ajuram	Petrocelinum sativum
Pepper (white)	Dipoive (blan)	Poivre blanc	Mirch	Piper nigrum
Pepper (black)	Dipoive (noir)	Poivre noir	Kali mirch	Piper nigrum
Salt	Sel de cuisine	Sel	Nimak	Sodium chloride
Sesame seed	Gingeli	Gingeli	Til	Sesamun indicum
Tamarind	Tamarin	Tamarin	Imli	Tamarindicus indica
Turmeric	Safran	Curcuma	Haldi	Curcuma longa

Abbreviations

gms or grms	=	gram
kg	=	kilogram
cl	=	centilitre
ml	=	millilitre
cm	=	centimetre
mm	=	millimetre

Index To Dishes

Acknowledgements

I would like to thank

  (i) Miss Floryse Lamy for translating into English from the original French Version: "La Vraie Cuisine Mauricienne".

  (ii) Mr Ronald Bégué for all photographs.

  (iii) Mr Jean-Daniel Marie for graphics.

  (iv) Miss Marie-Claude Pointu for typing work.

  (v) Mr Clifford Colimalay and Miss Sadhna Ramlallah for invaluable technical advice.

  (vi) Last but not least, my wife Michèle and my children Carine, Nadine and Guito, for all the help and encouragement in preparing. . . . and tasting all the dishes!

Guy Félix
October 1988.